AMERICA'S HOMELESS

Numbers, Characteristics, and Programs that Serve Them

URBAN INSTITUTE REPORT 89–3

Martha R. Burt
Barbara E. Cohen

THE URBAN INSTITUTE PRESS

Washington, D.C.

July 1989

THE URBAN INSTITUTE PRESS
2100 M Street, N.W.
Washington, D.C. 20037

Library of Congress Cataloging in Publication Data

America's Homeless: Numbers, Characteristics, and
Programs that Serve Them

1. Homeless persons--United States. 2. Homeless
persons--Services for--United States. 3. Homeless
persons--Government policy--United States. I. Cohen,
Barbara E. II. Title. III. Series.

HV4505.B87   1989   362.5'0973   89-9141

(Urban Institute Reports; 89-3, ISSN 0897-7399)

ISBN 0-87766-472-2
ISBN 0-87766-471-4 (casebound)

Printed in the United States of America.

1 2 3 4 5 6 7 8 9

Distributed by University Press of America

4720 Boston Way   3 Henrietta Street
Lanham, MD 20706   London WC2E 8LU ENGLAND

▥ URBAN INSTITUTE REPORTS

are designed to provide rapid dissemination of research and policy findings. Each report contains timely information and is rigorously reviewed to uphold the highest standards of policy research and analysis.

The Urban Institute is a nonprofit policy research and educational organization established in Washington, D.C., in 1968. Its staff investigates the social and economic problems confronting the nation and government policies and programs designed to alleviate such problems. The Institute disseminates significant findings of its research through the publications program of its Press. The Institute has two goals for work in each of its research areas: to help shape thinking about societal problems and efforts to solve them, and to improve government decisions and performance by providing better information and analytic tools.

Through work that ranges from broad conceptual studies to administrative and technical assistance, Institute researchers contribute to the stock of knowledge available to public officials and private individuals and groups concerned with formulating and implementing more efficient and effective government policy.

Conclusions or opinions expressed in Institute publications are those of the authors and do not necessarily reflect the views of other staff members, officers or trustees of the Institute, advisory groups, or any organizations that provide financial support to the Institute.

ACKNOWLEDGMENTS

A great many people and organizations helped make possible this wide-ranging report on America's homeless and attempts to assist them. The information here was condensed from three earlier reports, and also includes some new analyses. The first, a national study of homeless people and the facilities that provide them with shelter and food, was carried out for the U.S. Department of Agriculture's Food and Nutrition Service (Contract nos. FNS 53-3198-6-41 and FNS 53-3198-7-101). The second, an examination of state funding and activities related to homelessness in six states, was sponsored by the Interagency Council on the Homeless (Department of Housing and Urban Development Contract no. HC-5743). The third project reviewed available studies estimating the size of the homeless population and describing its characteristics, and was made possible under contract with the U.S. Department of Agriculture as part of its work with the Interagency Council on the Homeless (Contract no. FNS 53-3198-7-101).

Studies such as these, carried out across many cities and states, require the cooperation and assistance of many people: state and local government officials, advocates, providers, and homeless individuals. The quality of information available from these studies owes a great deal to these people.

Many people participated in data collection and analysis of the national study. Nancy Chapman of Chapman Associates contributed significantly as a consultant on nutritional aspects of the study. The sample design and the development and analysis of the sample weights were performed by Genevieve Kenney of The Urban Institute; Edward Bryant of Westat; and Brenda Cox of Research Triangle Institute (RTI), which under subcontract to The Urban Institute was responsible for selection, screening, and interviewing of homeless respondents, and prepared the raw data files from these interviews, with input from Martin Frankel of the National Opinion Research Center. Others at The Urban Institute who participated in the project include Alan Abramson, Dorothy Bell, Ken Danty, Sonja Drumgoole, Amina Elmi, Therese van Houten, Bill Marton, Emily McDonnell, Debbie Meiselman, Ronni Schwartz, Mildred Woodhouse, and Regina Yudd. Allen Duffer of RTI supervised the data collection that was completed under subcontract.

Linda Esrov of the Food and Nutrition Service actively participated in the development of the research design and analysis while serving as Project Officer under the first contract, as well as afterwards. Manuel de la Puente, the Project Officer under the second contract, and Linda Esrov contributed to the preparation of a final report. Others from the Food and Nutrition Service who have made contributions to the study include Melody Bacha, Carol Olander, Linda Basham, Mark Johnston, Lynn Jordan and Christy Schmidt.

Many people contributed to the study of homelessness in six states. Lynn Burbridge, Pam Holcomb, Janet Kahn, Eric Patashnik, Therese van Houten, and Regina Yudd participated in data collection and write-up. Guidance and review were received from Cassandra Moore and Michael Brintnall of the Interagency Council on the Homeless. Many people in the six states visited helped with setting up interviews, opening doors, and contributed and a great deal of important information.

The study would not have been possible without the cooperation of the local coordinators of services for the homeless providers at shelters and soup kitchens visited, homeless individuals, and administrators of local food stamp programs.

Finally, Susan Kalish improved the manuscript considerably with her editing.

CONTENTS

ABSTRACT

This report brings together findings from three recent research projects by The Urban Institute and adds some new analyses. Drawing on a nationally representative sample of interviews with homeless users of services and service providers in large cities, it provides new data on the number of homeless people, how they fare in the homeless condition, and the type and extent of services available to them. The report also explores what various states and localities are doing to provide emergency services to homeless people, to help people get out of homelessness, and to prevent homelessness. The report finds that, despite the great growth of services in the 1980s, existing amounts of emergency food and shelter meet only about half the need. Services that could help people work their way out of their homeless condition and government programs to prevent homelessness are not well developed. Although many workable approaches to addressing the problem can be found, the levels of funding and interest in finding solutions to the problems of homeless people vary greatly among different states. The data clearly show that--despite great growth of services in the 1980s and the massive efforts of food and shelter providers--current levels of resources are not meeting the need for emergency food and shelter. With an estimated 500,000 to 600,000 homeless people in this country at any given time, study findings demonstrate that homelessness is not a local problem--it is a national problem of severe proportions.

This report summarizes information from three recent research projects by The Urban Institute and adds some new analyses. It provides much new information on the situation of America's homeless and on efforts being made to help them. Much of the information comes from the first nationally representative survey of homeless people and providers in large cities, performed by The Urban Institute in March 1987. This survey provides new estimates of the numbers of homeless people, information about the history and characteristics of the homeless population, and takes a careful look at eating patterns of the homeless. It also describes the activities and sources of funding of programs that provide emergency food and shelter. In addition, the report includes information on what various states and localities are doing to provide emergency services to homeless people, to help people get out of homelessness, and to prevent homelessness.

HOW MANY HOMELESS ARE THERE ?

Estimates of the numbers of homeless people vary according to the definition of homelessness and the types of places enumerators visit to obtain a count. In March 1987, The Urban Institute interviewed 1,704 homeless adults in 20 cities to obtain a nationally representative random sample of homeless adults who used soup kitchens and shelters in cities of 100,000 population or more. This project created the first nationally representative data set that comes from interviews with the homeless themselves. These data lay the groundwork for national estimates and will facilitate inter-city comparisons. Children accompanying adults were not interviewed directly. For comparative purposes, a smaller group of interviews were conducted with homeless persons who do not use services.

The study estimates that in cities of 100,000+ population across the country, in March of 1987, there were 229,000 homeless people that used services--37 per 10,000 population. Further projections put the number of homeless people nationally at 496,000--600,000 in March 1987. These figures are approximately double the number of homeless estimated by the Department of Housing and Urban Development (HUD) in 1983. Since data suggest that the number of people homeless during the course of a year is approximately double the number homeless at any given time, these figures imply that more than one million persons in the U.S. were homeless at some time in 1987. If these homeless people were to gather in one place, they would constitute the ninth largest city in the United States.

CHARACTERISTICS AND EATING PATTERNS OF THE HOMELESS

The interviews indicate that many homeless people have a number of disabilities and other strikes against them. Single homeless people tend to have more troubled histories than adults who have children with them. A comparative sample of homeless who do not use services indicates they fare even less well than those who do use services. Among the estimated 229,000 homeless adults and children that use services in cities of 100,000 population or more, the following facts stand out:

✦ *Family structure.* Adults make up 194,000 of the service-using homeless; children accompanying them make up the remaining 35,000. Ten percent of homeless households are families with children.

✦ *Gender.* Most of the homeless (81 percent) are male.

✦ *Race.* Fifty-four percent are nonwhite. Homeless people are three to four times as likely to be black and slightly more likely to be Hispanic than the general population.

✦ *Education.* Forty-eight percent have not graduated from high school (compared with 19 percent for all U.S. adults).

✦ *Length of homelessness.* Homeless persons tend to be homeless for substantial periods (median of 10 months for the entire sample). One-fifth have been homeless three months or less, while a like proportion have been homeless four years or more. Households with children are likely to be homeless for shorter periods (41 percent for three months or less).

✦ *Income.* The average monthly income per person was $135, less than one-third of the federal poverty level. Men were more likely to report income from handouts; women from means-tested government benefits such as food stamps, Aid to Families with Dependent Children (AFDC), and General Assistance (GA).

✦ *Work history.* The homeless have been jobless longer than they have been homeless. About half had not had a steady job (three months with the same employer) in more than two years.

✦ *Health.* Over half (56 percent) reported at least one health problem, including 15 percent with joint problems, 15 percent with high blood pressure, and 10 percent with problems walking. Physical health problems may have contributed to becoming homeless.

✦ *Mental health.* One-fifth reported a history of mental hospitalization and a similar proportion had attempted suicide.

Half rated high enough on a scale of depression and demoralization to indicate the need for immediate treatment. Women with children with them reported a much lower rate of mental hospitalization, but still had five times the normal rate of suicide attempts.

✦ *Institutionalization.* One-third had been patients in a detoxification or alcohol/drug treatment center. Sixty percent of the single men, 22 percent of the single women, and 15 percent of the women with children had spent more than three or four days in a county jail (possibly some as a direct result of being homeless). In addition, 29 percent of single men, but just 2 percent of all women, had served time in a state or federal prison.

The diets for homeless people interviewed are not adequate, either in terms of frequency and regularity of eating, quality of food, or variety of foods eaten. Three out of four homeless people eat only two meals a day or less, while 36 percent go one day or more per week without any food. They also eat relatively few servings of food: a median of nine servings of all foods per day, compared with a USDA-recommended 15-25 servings just for essential, nutritious foods. The day before the interview, 65 percent of interviewees said they had eaten no milk or milk products, 43 percent had eaten no fruits or vegetables, 30 percent had eaten no grain products, and 20 percent had eaten no meat or meat alternates.

The great majority (88 percent) of adults with children were women. Homeless families had been homeless for a median of 4.5 months and without work for a median of 20 months. About half the families were receiving food stamps, and about two-thirds were receiving AFDC benefits and/or General Assistance. Homeless families tend to be more consistent users of services than single homeless people. The typical diet of homeless adults with children with them compares poorly with that of the average American: they eat fewer meals per day and are more likely to go whole days without food. The interviews obtained no information on the diets of homeless children directly.

CHARACTERISTICS OF SOUP KITCHENS AND SHELTERS

The amounts of emergency food and shelter available to the homeless do not meet the need. In March 1987 in U.S. cities of over 100,000 population, there were approximately 120,000 shelter beds available, and about 321,000 meals per day were served to the homeless. Looking at just the number of homeless who do avail themselves of services, the number of 229,000 available shelter beds amounts to slightly less than half the estimated number of homeless people. The number of meals available would provide an average of only 1.4 meals per day for each homeless person. This gap between services and need does not account for the additional unknown number of urban homeless people who do not use services at all. These severe shortages exist, despite the enormous growth over the 1980s of shelters and soup kitchens. Sixty-three percent of these facilities started operating in the 1980s. Only 15 percent have been in business 21 years or more.

As of winter 1987 the Institute's estimates indicated that there were almost 3,000 providers of meals and/or shelter for the homeless in cities of 100,000 population or more. The majority are church affiliated. In addition to meals and shelter, services such as clothing and health care referrals, bathing facilities, mail receiving, and social work/counseling may be offered. Most providers are small or medium-sized: only 23 percent serve more than 100 clients per meal or per night. Almost half are shelters that serve their residents at least one meal a day, another 41 percent are soup kitchens. Only 12 percent are shelters serving no meals.

Over half the shelters that serve meals provide three meals per day. In contrast, almost three-quarters of soup kitchens serve only one meal per day. Meals provided tended to be varied in in the food served, and of high nutritional content, apparently reflecting provider policy to make their meals, which might be the only food their clients consume in a day, of high nutritional value.

Government has become a bigger player in services for the homeless over the last few years, mainly in the area of financial support for shelters. But individuals, religious congregations, charitable organizations, United Way, businesses, and foundations still provide most of the labor, goods, and services.

A 1989 HUD report indicates that 65 percent of shelter operating expenses came from government, and only 35 percent came from private sources--a reversal of the 1983 public-private funding ratio. Federal funds available since late 1987 through the Stewart B. McKinney Homeless Assistance Act are responsible for part of this increase in government support, but state and local governments contribute between half and three-fourths of government funding.

When asked about their first or second largest source of food 56 percent named purchase, 39 percent private donations, 35 percent USDA commodities, and 34 percent food banks. Fifty-nine percent of meal providers counted individuals as their first or second largest source of cash income; 45 percent reported getting some cash from government. Thirty-five percent of meal providers operate with no paid staff, and all make extensive use of volunteer labor.

STATE AND FEDERAL ACTIVITIES

In general, government has been a latecomer in providing financial or programmatic support for homeless programs.

The states in which government has done the most appear to be states with strong local voluntary services for the homeless and statewide coalitions of service providers and advocates who have pressured government to act.

Government action is needed both short term, to fund emergency and transitional services for homeless people, and long term, to prevent homelessness. Government also has other potential--to service a planning and coordinating function, to develop a sophisticated understanding of what is needed to eliminate homelessness, to create needed resources through its legislative powers, and to allocate these resources where they are needed. The Urban Institute visited six states to describe state programs and activities for the homeless, to ascertain levels of commitment to homeless issues, and identify innovative approaches to the problem. The six states are California, Connecticut, Georgia, New Mexico, Ohio, and Wisconsin. Highlights of the study are:

✦ State housing agencies are not taking the lead in coordinating McKinney Act funding from HUD. This points out a built-in difficulty of housing authorities to consider social goods other than investment safety when making housing investment decisions.

✦ States with well-developed programs for the homeless have been most successful in obtaining federal funds, in part because they can meet the matching-fund stipulations of the McKinney Act.

✦ Federal funding sources for food programs include the Temporary Emergency Food Assistance Program and the Emergency Food and Shelter Program.

✦ A major private initiative, the Health Care for the Homeless Program of the Robert Wood Johnson Foundation, has demonstrated the ability to provide successful accessible health services for the homeless.

✦ To address the lack of affordable housing, states and localities have developed rent subsidy programs, rent negotiation programs, and public/private programs to refurbish single room occupancy (SRO) units. They have also increased bonding authority to develop low-income housing, through legislative action and initiatives.

✦ In states with one major urban center, the public and state legislatures tend to consider homelessness as a local problem of that city and are reluctant to fund programs.

✦ States vary in the levels of interest and resources devoted to the homeless problem. In two states visited, mental health issues dominate the provision of services for the homeless, with insufficient focus on other types of homeless people.

Several barriers to the receipt of services were identified: the lack of case management, a lack of information about programs, a lack of outreach, difficult and confusing application forms, long waiting times, and office locations inconvenient to shelters. Requirements of a fixed address to qualify for services or to enroll children in school also block homeless people from receiving transitional services.

The primary federal legislation aimed at the homeless problem, the McKinney Act, focuses too heavily on bricks and mortar for emergency shelters, while failing to address the shortage of permanent low-income housing. Moreover, in some states, would-be applicants for McKinney funds have been frustrated by truncated application periods, complex paperwork requirements, and bureaucratic rigidities, which make it difficult to arrange a comprehensive package of housing and services fo the homeless in emergency and transitional situations. Many respondents spoke in favor of a new, block grant approach. Prohibitions in state constitutions on state funding of housing form another barrier. Yet, another barrier arises when state policy and federal policy conflict, as has occurred in Ohio on the issue of group homes versus scattered site housing for the mentally ill. Moreover, inflation has increased construction costs, and in some states, the shortage of low-income housing is part of a more general housing shortage.

DIRECTIONS FOR FUTURE POLICY

The causes of homelessness are many, and solutions must emerge from all sectors--government at all levels, the nonprofit and voluntary sectors, and the business community. Three kinds of solutions are required:

+ the emergency response--to provide food, shelter, and health care to people already homeless,

+ transitional programs--to help people already homeless to get back into permanent housing and to develop a better capacity for self-sufficiency, and

+ prevention--the development of public policy that strives to keep people from becoming homeless in the first place.

Of these, the first approach is well developed (although arrangements do not meet the need), primarily through the efforts of the voluntary and religious sectors. The second approach is less well developed and, since it requires a substantial amount of funding and professional staffing, government will have to be a primary supporter. The third approach is least developed of all. Current federal housing programs and policies fail to address the need for permanent low-income housing. Yet, many valuable models of innovative low-income housing projects exist. The voluntary sector will have to continue in its key advocacy role--keeping the heat on government and voters--to strengthen the emergency food and shelter network that is already in place, to build transition services, and to build up the stock of low-income housing to prevent homelessness.

The existence of so many homeless people strongly suggests that there has been a breakdown in basic systems in this country that are supposed to safeguard the populace from complete impoverishment. This report shows that--despite great growth of services over the 1980s and the efforts of providers--today's levels of resources and current public policies are not meeting the need. This study documents that homelessness is a national problem of severe proportions.

Chapter One

INTRODUCTION

Currently there is intense public policy interest in the homeless. The U.S. has always been "home" to winos, tramps, hobos, and skid row bums, as well as to entire uprooted cultures, such as the migrants created by the Midwest dust bowl in the 1930s. However, since the early 1980s the general public has become increasingly aware that many people cannot house themselves, and the phenomenon of homelessness has become generally recognized. The terms *homeless* and *homelessness* first came into prominence during the recession of 1981-82. Since then many reports have described increasing homelessness, the changing nature of the homeless population, and the expanding array of services emerging to help the homeless.

GOVERNMENT INITIATIVES

The federal government has taken several actions in response to homelessness. The first came in 1983 with the Emergency Food and Shelter Program contained in the Jobs Stimulus Act of 1983 (P.L. 98-8). Known as FEMA after the Federal Emergency Management Administration, the federal agency charged with responsibility for administering it, this program is run through a national board of nonprofit agencies with extensive experience in programs for the homeless. The national board's composition is a clear reflection of Congress' recognition that the nonprofit sector and volunteers were (as they still are) the front line in providing services and support for the homeless. In 1983 three-fourths of the resources of this program went toward food assistance; by 1989 more than half of the resources were committed to shelter services. Further, The Emergency Food and Shelter Program supplies the only significant resources for prevention of homelessness; approximately 60 percent of its shelter funding goes for emergency rent, mortgage, or utility payments that prevent eviction.

The Stewart B. McKinney Homeless Assistance Act of 1987 (P.L. 100-77) was the next congressional effort to provide direct support for emergency shelters. The McKinney Act also authorized and appropriated money for a wide range of other programs designed to assist homeless persons with emergency needs and also to provide necessary support and training to help them make the transition out of homelessness. These programs cover primary health care, mental health care, alcohol and other drug abuse services, education for both adults and children, job training, community services, and programs specifically for homeless veterans. Chapter 5 of this report describes the effects of the availability of federal funding through the McKinney Act on programs and activities for the homeless in six states, and also describes some of the problems with implementing the act from the state and local perspective.

Other congressional action taken in the Food Security Act of 1985, the Homeless Eligibility Clarification Act of 1986, and the McKinney Act of 1987 directly focused on the food needs of the homeless by stipulating changes and clarifications in the regulations governing the Food Stamp Program to make that program more accessible to the homeless. The Homeless Eligibility Clarification Act also made other federal benefit programs, such as Aid to Families with Dependent Children (AFDC) and Medicaid, more accessible to homeless people. In addition, the Hunger Relief Act of 1988 added $40 million of federal money to expand the availability and improve the quality of shelter and soup kitchen meals for the homeless.

Despite the recent explosion of federal attention to programs for the homeless, government at all levels is a late entrant in the support for services to the homeless. In the early part of the 1980s private sector resources were the mainstay of services for the homeless. Even in the late 1980s the U.S. Department of Housing and Urban Development (HUD) (1989) estimates that private resources supply about one-third of the cash and most of the labor for shelter services. For food services the proportions are even more skewed in the direction of private and voluntary support, with government at all levels supplying less than half of the cash for soup kitchen and shelter meal operations (Burt and Cohen 1988b). Chapter 4 describes the growth of services for the homeless and their sources of support. Federal government actions lag behind efforts in some states and localities severely affected by homelessness, but have served as a catalyst in some states which had no state initiatives prior to the passage of the McKinney Act in July 1987.

Homelessness has become a public policy concern, a major focus of private charity, and a much-debated public issue. However, accurate information about the homeless and services for them has not kept pace with this interest. This report makes available much new information on America's homeless and the efforts being made to assist them. It consolidates the most important and timely findings of three projects recently completed at The Urban Institute--interviews with a nationally representative sample of the urban homeless along with an examination of the operations of soup kitchens and shelters; a six-state examination of policies and activities concerning the homeless, including a description of how states are using federal funds in this area; and, a review of previous studies based on interviews with homeless people in different cities.

The first project (reported in *Feeding the Homeless,* Burt and Cohen, 1988) was the first national study based on probability sampling methods to examine the operations of soup kitchens and shelters and to interview randomly selected homeless individuals using these facilities in large

U.S. cities. This effort produced national estimates of the size of the homeless population to be based on probability sampling techniques, described the characteristics of homeless adults, and documented the sources of support and the scope of activities of soup kitchens and shelters. All these data have great policy relevance.

The second project examined state funding and activities related to homelessness in six states. It investigated how state government and other organizations were using federal funding under the McKinney Act, and what barriers exist for both service receipt by homeless people and service development by interested organizations.

The third project was smaller in scope. It reviewed several studies that describe characteristics of homeless individuals based on interviews with the homeless, and also examined previous efforts to count or estimate the numbers of homeless people. All of the interview-based studies and most of the estimate attempts had been conducted in single cities. These earlier studies yielded great variation in results, which frustrated efforts to extrapolate findings from one city to another or to use them to develop coherent programs addressing the many needs of the homeless. Our review analyzed the reasons for these variations. Using the findings of the Institute's national study of the homeless, just described, it becomes possible for the first time to account for these variations and to discern the central tendency among them.

This information can help resolve the many controversies that hinder the formulation of adequate public policy. Much of the controversy surrounding homelessness focuses on the question of numbers. Questions here include: How many homeless people are there in the United States on any single night? How many people experience homelessness during a particular time period, for example, one year? Has the population of homeless people grown in recent years, and, if so, by how much? What proportion of the homeless avail themselves of the services offered? Chapter 2 of this report summarizes recent efforts to count the homeless, and sets forth new estimates of the numbers of urban homeless service users, and of all homeless persons in the U.S.

Other policy debates concern the nature of the homeless population--the age, gender, and family status of the homeless as well as their levels of education, job history, and health status. Therefore chapter 3 presents the Institute's findings from our national sample on selected characteristics of homeless people, noting why each characteristic may be important for policy. Among these findings we include current service utilization patterns of homeless people, which reflect service availability and unmet need. The report also includes a comparison of our national findings with parallel statistics from 14 local studies that interviewed homeless individuals. The variations in these local statistics have been the cause of much uncertainty about the nature of the homeless population; we can now reduce much of this uncertainty. Chapter 4 reports on the interviews conducted with emergency food and shelter providers in cities of 100,000[+] population. This information provides additional insight into the question of unmet needs.

Since the response to homelessness for most of this decade has been at the local level, a dearth of information exists nationally that describes either what programs have been tried, or what programs work. Chapter 5 of this report describes what is being done by certain states and localities to address the problem of homelessness at various levels, including emergency services (shelter, food, medical care), transitional services for those already homeless, and services and programs to prevent homelessness. It details how federal resources are being used (or failing to be used), provision of state resources, and state legislation and state coordination efforts. It discusses barriers to service receipt by homeless individuals and barriers to program development, as seen by state government and local private sector individuals involved with homeless issues.

Chapter Two

HOW MANY HOMELESS ARE THERE ?

Definitions lie at the heart of debates about how many people are homeless. The definition of who is homeless varies somewhat with every study and every report. The McKinney Act provides the core definition for this report. The act defines as homeless:

> (1) An individual who lacks a fixed, regular, and adequate nighttime residence; and (2) an individual who has a primary nighttime residence that is (a) a supervised publicly or privately operated shelter designed to provide temporary living accommodations (including welfare hotels, congregate shelters, and transitional housing for the mentally ill), (b) an institution that provides a temporary residence for individuals intended to be institutionalized, or, (c) a public or private place not designated for, or ordinarily used as, a regular sleeping accommodation for human beings (P.L.100-77, July 22, 1987).

The simplest definition of homelessness is "without shelter on the night of measurement." Someone using a shelter for the homeless on the night of measurement is assumed to be "without shelter."

Regardless of any official definition, all estimates of the size of the homeless population are based on specific studies. Any given study defines in practical terms who is homeless in practical terms through its decisions about where to seek interviews with potentially homeless persons. The greater number of types of locations one visits to find the homeless, the more inclusive one's working definition of who is homeless, and the larger one's estimate of the number of homeless persons. However, at present data do not exist that can specify precisely how estimated numbers would increase or decline as a consequence of including or omitting particular types of locations or individuals from the definition of homelessness.

If a study includes battered women's shelters, then battered women and their children will emerge as a category of the homeless; if the researchers do not include battered women's shelters, then women and their families in these shelters are not counted among the homeless. The same is true for families in welfare hotels or individuals using vouchers to live in single room occupancy (SRO) hotels; if the hotels are included in the research design, their occupants are included in the count of the homeless, otherwise they are not. Minors (runaway and homeless youth) are not accepted at most shelters for the homeless and shelters for runaway and homeless youth which do serve minors have usually not been included among the shelters visited in homeless surveys. Therefore runaway and homeless youth have not usually figured in counts of the homeless. Nevertheless, by the McKinney Act definition, all of these types of individuals would be considered homeless.

Two studies (City of Boston Emergency Shelter Commission 1983; Goplerud 1987) extended the search for the homeless even further. Researchers located individuals in institutions (such as detoxification centers, community mental health centers, jails, alcohol and drug treatment programs, and hospitals) who had nowhere to go upon release, and counted them among the homeless even though they currently resided in an institution. A study by Roth et al. (1985) included in its definition of the homeless individuals and household units who temporarily resided with family and friends ("doubled up") as long as they did not *intend* to stay for more than 45 days, even when they had spent every night for the past month in the doubled-up household and might *in fact* stay more than 45 days. Two studies (City of Boston Emergency Shelter Commission 1983; Hirschl and Momeni 1988) also reported counts of doubled-up households but did not include them in their count of the homeless. Temporarily institutionalized persons with no fixed address clearly fit the McKinney Act definition of a homeless person. However, whether doubled-up households fit the definition depends on one's interpretation of "fixed, regular, and adequate nighttime residence."

The street population--undomiciled individuals who do not use any shelters--clearly fits any definition of the homeless, but many studies do not attempt to interview them. The section that follows describes how researchers have attempted to estimate the size of this non-service-using segment of the homeless population.

ESTIMATES OF THE SIZE OF THE HOMELESS POPULATION

Problems of Measurement and Alternative Solutions

No one knows exactly how many homeless people there are in the United States. Those who try to measure the homeless population encounter enormous problems. First, it is difficult to include in the count homeless persons who do not use shelters or other services. The potential for duplicate counts also exists. Reports that do not clearly identify whether their numbers refer to individuals or to households introduce further confusion.

People who use shelters are the easiest part of the homeless population to enumerate. Researchers can identify almost all available shelters (including hotels and motels used for that purpose) and the number of beds they have available. Numbers of homeless sheltered on a given night can then be estimated by summing the number of beds available and adjusting for the number of beds actually occupied on a given night. Estimates of the numbers of homeless are frequently formed on this basis.

Some studies spread a wider net to enumerate the service-using homeless by including not only shelters but soup kitchens and daytime drop-in or warming centers.

However, many people who eat at soup kitchens are not homeless; many people who eat at soup kitchens are homeless and also use shelters. Drop-in centers may also serve a variety of users. When a study uses several types of facilities in making its estimates of the size of the homeless population, care must be taken to avoid duplicate counting, and to count only those service users who are homeless. Using provider estimates of the "numbers turned away" on an average night also has the problem of duplicate counting, since someone may be turned away from more than one shelter, or may be turned away from one shelter but eventually spend the night at another shelter.

The hardest subgroup of the homeless population to enumerate accurately consists of people who do not use any services. Because no one knows the size or characteristics of this population, most standard sampling procedures will not yield results that can be generalized or weighted to represent the whole population. One approach is to take a census--to attempt to count everyone who is homeless on the streets or in public places (including abandoned buildings, tent cities, cars and other vehicles, parts of the highway or subway systems, and transportation depots) on a single night. This method involves the use of many enumerators who cover the entire city on the specified night, approaching everyone they see and determining whether or not that person is homeless. Quite a number of cities have made this effort, including Boston, Chicago, Fairfax County (Virginia), Nashville, New York City, Pittsburgh, Phoenix, and Washington, D.C.

A recent study of the homeless in Chicago and another in California used a variation on the census approach (Rossi et al. 1986; Vernez et al. 1988). These studies sampled city blocks, each of which had been designated as having a high, medium, or low probability of containing homeless persons. Since blocks could be enumerated and then selected with a known probability, this methodology permitted an estimate of the size of the total street homeless population without having to locate and count every homeless person.

Even though the census approach and its variants make every effort to locate and count all of the homeless persons "on the street" on the census night, it is still likely that some homeless persons are overlooked. Since spending the night on the streets is dangerous, homeless persons exercise considerable ingenuity to find some secure and unobserved location in which to sleep. Therefore, even with a census, the issue will always remain as to how many people the census missed, and how much the census count should be inflated to arrive at the actual number of homeless.

Other approaches to estimating the number of homeless include a reliance on provider or other expert opinion, or on taking the number of individuals receiving shelter and applying a multiplier factor to adjust for the number of unsheltered homeless. The first HUD study (Department of Housing and Urban Development 1984) did both. It relied on expert opinion in the 60 metropolitan areas included in the study for one estimate; it then took the known number of shelter beds available nationally and multiplied by a ratio derived from studies in Boston, Phoenix and Pittsburgh to obtain a different estimate.

However, among different cities that have taken actual street counts which can be compared to the sheltered population, the ratios of street homeless to sheltered homeless vary enormously. In a recent review and summary of eight methodologically sound studies in different cities (GAO 1988, table 2.4), the federal General Accounting Office found the highest ratio to be 144 street persons to every 100 sheltered persons in the fall of 1985 in Chicago (Rossi et al. 1986). The lowest ratios in the GAO report were 6 street to 100 sheltered persons in Fairfax County, VA (Goplerud 1987) and 7 street to 100 sheltered persons in Nashville in winter 1985 (Weigand 1985). No studies, other than Rossi et al., found more people on the streets than in the shelters; even in the Rossi et al., study, the finding for winter was only 35 people on the streets for every 100 in shelters--in sharp contrast to their findings for the fall data collection period. GAO reported ratios from other studies of 14, 15, 21, 32, 39, 64 and 75 street people to 100 sheltered people.

Given these figures, it is hardly a straightforward task to select a multiplier on which one could get consensus from the diverse groups and agencies interested in the homeless issue. The studies reviewed by GAO cover time periods from 1983 through 1987, and were conducted in cities that began their buildup of homeless services at very different times. Given the growth of shelter services in this country during the past five years, it is not likely that these ratios have remained the same. One likely possibility is that larger and larger proportions of the homeless use shelter services as more and more shelters are developed. Thus shelter operators, when asked as they were in several surveys conducted by the U.S. Conference of Mayors (1984, 1986a, 1986b, 1987), might accurately say that the numbers of sheltered homeless have increased dramatically, but it might also be true that the total number of homeless persons has changed little.

HOW MANY HOMELESS ?

With a clear acknowledgment of the inherent measurement problems, then, let us first look at the best earlier attempts to estimate the size of the homeless population and then at the results of the Institute's study. We reviewed 14 studies estimating the size of either local or national homeless populations. Only studies with a clearly described methodology were reviewed, which included all existing efforts to construct national estimates. All of these national estimates except the Institute's estimates were based on HUD's first report (Department of Housing and Urban Development 1984). Selected local studies were included if their methodology was clear and if they applied to a clearly defined population base that could provide the denominator necessary to create a homeless rate. These studies used different definitions, which might also affect their estimates of population size and growth.

Estimates of Local Homeless Populations

A number of local studies conducted in single cities took a census or otherwise estimated the size of the homeless population on a given night. We compared these figures to the city population to create a *homeless* rate (the number of homeless persons per 10,000 population). The homeless rate provides a way of comparing results across cities of different sizes. It also provides a basis for generalizing to other cities which have not themselves conducted a count, or to the whole country.

Table 2.1 compares the findings of these studies. It displays the estimated number of homeless persons, the population of the city or jurisdiction in the year closest to the time of the estimate, and the homeless rate for jurisdictions that have conducted enumerations of homeless persons. As the last column of table 2.1 clearly shows, the homeless rate varies considerably between jurisdictions. The highest rates (between 37 and 50 per 10,000) were reported for Boston and the District of Columbia. Moderate rates (between 13 and 17 per 10,000) were reported for the other cities in the table, with the exception of Chicago.[1] Estimates for suburban (Fairfax County, a suburban county adjacent to Washington, D.C.) and rural or mixed urban-rural areas (rural Ohio) are below 10 persons per 10,000, as are recent estimates for three California counties.

Estimates of the National Homeless Population

Table 2.2 gives the results of several efforts to estimate the total number of homeless persons nationally prior to the Institute's research. The first such study, conducted by HUD in 1983 (Department of Housing and Urban Development 1984), developed an estimate of 250,000-350,000 as the "most reliable range." The HUD report translated these figures into homeless rates of 13.0, 12.0 and 6.5 per 10,000 for large, medium, and small metropolitan areas, respectively. All of the other estimates

TABLE 2.1   HOMELESS RATES FOR DIFFERENT CITIES
ESTIMATED FROM STUDIES WITH STREET COUNTS

Jurisdiction	Year data collected	Estimated number of homeless[a]	City population (1,000s)	Homeless rate (N/10,000)
Boston	1983	2,115	571	37.0
		2,767[b]	571	48.5
	1986	2,863	574	49.9
Chicago	1985-6	2,200	2,992	7.4
District of Columbia	1985	2,652	623	41.1
Nashville	1983-4	791[c]	462	17.1
Phoenix	1982	1,264	824	15.3
Pittsburgh	1983	549	403	13.6
Fairfax County, Virginia	1987	426	670	6.8
		654[c]	670	9.8
Ohio - 16 Rural Counties	1985	261	1,091	2.4
California (Rand)	1987			
Alameda		817	1,209	6.8
Orange		764	2,167	3.5
Yolo		71	126	5.6

Sources: City of Boston Emergency Shelter Commission (1983); City of Boston (1986); Robinson (1985); Weigand (1985); Brown et al. (1983); Winograd (1983); Goplerud (1987); Roth et al. (1985); Vernez et al. (1988).

a. These figures include both sheltered and unsheltered homeless. Some studies gave figures for homeless people actually observed on the streets, and also gave adjusted estimates based on some assumptions about how many homeless people were missed in the street counts. All figures in this column refer to the numbers actually observed.
b. With homeless persons in institutions added to first number (jails, hospitals, community mental health centers, detoxification centers, drug and alcohol treatment centers).
c. Average of 4 counts, one during each season during a whole year.

TABLE 2.2   PREVIOUS ESTIMATES OF THE NATIONAL HOMELESS
RATE

Study[a]	Estimated number of homeless	Homeless rate (N/10,000)
HUD Report (for 1983)		
Full range	192,000 - 586,000	8.1 - 25.0[a]
Most reliable range	250,000 - 350,000	10.7 - 14.9[a]
Large metropolitan areas	150,000	13.0[b]
Medium metropolitan areas	41,000	12.0[b]
Small metropolitan areas	19,000	6.5[b]
Non-metropolitan areas	44,000	7.8[a]
Revisions based on HUD numbers		
NBER-1 (for 1983)[c]	279,000	11.9[a]
NBER-2 (for 1985)[d]	343,000 - 363,000	14.4 - 15.2
ICF		
Total for United States as as whole in 1983	355,000	15.0[ae]
Projection to United States as a whole in 1987	735,000	30.5[af]

SOURCES: Department of Housing and Urban Development (1984);
Freeman and Hall (1987); Committee for Food and Shelter, Inc. (1987).
NOTE: NBER = National Bureau of Economic Research.
a. Rate calculated for this report.
b. Rate given in original report.
c. Augmented HUD figures by adding people in welfare hotels,
detoxification centers, battered women's shelters and shelters for runaway
and homeless youth for 1983.
d. Developed by applying growth rates for homeless individuals and for
families, obtained from studies in Boston and New York, to 1983 figures.
e. Calculations reported in Committee for Food and Shelter, Inc. (1987).
Rates for metropolitan areas use the populations within the city limits as
the denominator, rather than the entire population of the metropolitan
area. Rate for non-city parts of metropolitan areas and for non-
metropolitan areas was assumed to be 1/3 the city rate.
f. Projection for 1987 developed by increasing the 1983 total by 20 percent
a year, a multiplier without any empirical basis.

shown in table 2.2 are based on these most reliable range figures from this HUD study. The HUD estimates were derived using four different approaches. Some were based on provider estimates; others relied on the numbers of sheltered homeless augmented by use of a multiplier to estimate the non-sheltered homeless.

The National Bureau of Economic Research (NBER) recalculated the HUD numbers, making several different adjustments to accommodate some of the criticisms of HUD's methodology (Freeman and Hall 1987). Their re-estimation produced a number very close to the midpoint of HUD's most reliable range for 1983, and then projected the numbers to 1985 based on growth rates from studies in New York City and Boston. The NBER estimate for 1983 was 279,000, with a homeless rate of 11.9 per 10,000; its estimate for 1985 was 343,000-363,000, with a homeless rate of 14.4-15.2 per 10,000.

In a report for the Committee for Food and Shelter, Inc. (1987), staff from ICF, Inc., made another re-estimate based on HUD data. They made two major alterations in their approach. HUD had sampled entire metropolitan areas, which incorporate an area much larger than the city limits of urban centers. For example, the metropolitan area for Phoenix contains the city of Phoenix and all of its suburbs. In developing homeless rates, some critics (Appelbaum 1985a, 1985b) assumed that HUD had divided the estimate of the number of homeless in central cities by the entire population of the metropolitan area.[2]

Therefore, ICF's recalculation used the city population as the denominator for determining rates *for the cities*, even though HUD's estimates were for the metropolitan areas. This technique left both the non-metropolitan areas and the suburban areas outside the city limits without a projection of the homeless population. Based on several studies of non-urban populations, ICF assumed that the homeless rate outside of the city limits was one-third of the city rate. ICF's homeless population estimate of 355,000 (rate of 15.0 per 10,000) for 1984 is based on these assumptions.

Even with ICF's recalculation, its 1984 estimate of 355,000 is very close to the upper end of HUD's most reasonable range of 250,000-350,000. HUD's method spreads the estimate of the number of homeless over the population base of the entire metropolitan area, thus creating a lower rate but covering a larger population. ICF's method produces a higher rate for the homeless within the city limits, of 28/10,000 in 1984, but then estimates the homeless in the remainder of the metropolitan area using a rate 1/3 of the city rate, or 9/10,000. The end results of the two methods are relatively close. Finally, the figures from smaller jurisdictions summarized in table 2.1, which range from 2.4/10,000 to 6.8/10,000, suggest that ICF's assumption that the rate for areas outside the city limits should be 9/10,000 may overestimate the rate of homelessness in these areas.

ICF's projection of 735,000 homeless people in 1987 (30.5 per 10,000) increases the 1984 rate by 20 percent per year, although no adequate empirical basis exists for this 20 percent figure. Indeed, the only data that allow comparisons over time show little or no growth in the homeless population. Two Boston studies (City of Boston Emergency Shelter Commission 1983; City of Boston 1986) allow comparison between 1983 and 1986, and show a 1 percent growth in the homeless population during those years. Data collected at least semi-annually in Nashville during the five years from 1983-1987 show no growth in the homeless population, although the population does fluctuate from survey to survey (Lee 1988).

The Urban Institute Study: A New Statistical Basis for Estimating the Homeless Population

In 1987 The Urban Institute conducted the first national study to interview homeless individuals who used soup kitchens and shelters in U.S. cities of 100,000 population or more. The study included 1,704 in-person interviews conducted in March 1987 with a probability-based three-stage random sample of homeless adult service users in these cities. The city sample of 20 cities included with certainty the six cities with populations exceeding one million in 1984. The remaining 14 cities in the sample were selected from other cities of their size and region with a probability proportional to the size of their poverty population.

Providers of shelter or meals (N=381) were randomly selected from the universe of such facilities within the city limits of these cities, with a response rate of 84 percent. Homeless respondents were randomly selected from cooperating providers, with an interview completion rate of 88 percent. Data reported here are weighted to represent all service-using homeless adults in the universe of the 178 U.S. cities with populations of 100,000 or more in 1984.[3] The data base is extremely valuable because for the first time it allows researchers to transcend the biases inherent in local studies, and to develop reasonable national statistics of the homeless population.

Table 2.3 presents the Institute's estimate of the numbers of urban service-using homeless adults and children in March 1987. It also presents projections to the national homeless population, based on this estimate and coupled with a number of assumptions about the ratio of non-service users to service users and the rates of homelessness outside the city limits of large U.S. cities.

About 229,000 homeless persons in cities with population 100,000 or over used meal or shelter services at some time during a seven-day period in March 1987. Adults comprise 194,000 of this number; children accompanying these adults make up the remaining 35,000.[4]

This estimate applies only to homeless people who use soup kitchens and shelters in our nation's 178 largest cities in 41 states. To develop an estimate of the national homeless population one must make some assumptions: first, about the ratio of non-service users to service users in the cities in our study universe; second, about the rates of homelessness in the remainder of the U.S. in comparison to the city rates--assumed to be 1/3 of the city rate for the Metropolitan Statistical Area (MSA) population excluding the

TABLE 2.3   THE URBAN INSTITUTE'S ESTIMATES FOR URBAN
SERVICE-USING HOMELESS, AND PROJECTIONS
TO ALL HOMELESS IN THE UNITED STATES

Population	Estimated number of of homeless	Homeless rate (N/10,000)
Service-using homeless in cities of 100,000 or more (including children) in March 1987[a]	229,000	37.4
Projection to United States as a whole in March 1987, assuming 50 non-service users for every 100 service users[b]	567,000- 600,000	23.5- 24.9
Projection to United States as a whole in March 1987, assuming 20 non-service users for every 100 service users	496,000	20.6

a. A very broad confidence interval is associated with the adult
estimate of 194,000 ($\pm$ 42 percent, or $\pm$ 81,893); for the children's
estimate of 35,000 it is much smaller ($\pm$ 647, or 1.9 percent).
Please refer to Burt and Cohen (1988b), volume II, part 2, section
B for a detailed description of sampling and weighting issues that
contributed to this estimate.

b. The methods used to make this projection are detailed in Burt
(1988).

population of cities over 100,000, and 9/10,000 for the population outside of MSAs; and third, about the presence of children accompanying non-service-using adults in comparison to their presence among the service-using homeless.

The second row in table 2.3 shows the results of three projections, each based on an assumption that there are 50 non-service-using homeless adults for every 100 service-using homeless adults in large U.S. cities. The higher estimate (600,000) assumes that children are present among non-service users in the same proportion that they are present among homeless adults who only use soup kitchens (which is considerably less than their presence in the sheltered homeless population), and that the ratio of non-users to users is the same outside of our universe of cities as it is within that universe. The lower estimate (567,000) makes the same assumption about children among non-service users, but also assumes that the ratio of non-users to users outside of our city universe is one-half of the same ratio within the cities in our universe (or, a ratio of 25/100).

These assumptions err, if they do at all, on the generous side. Some of the studies report street-to-shelter ratios as high as 50/100 but more report lower ratios. In addition, the Institute's data include individuals who do not use shelters, but only use soup kitchens. In most other studies these people would be counted on the street side of the street-to-shelter ratio, whereas in our approach they are counted among the service users.

It is certainly reasonable to use a 50/100 ratio in making an estimate, but it is not unreasonable to wonder what the effects would be of using a lower ratio. The third row of table 2.3 shows one such alternative estimate. This estimate uses a ratio of 20/100 applied to jurisdictions of all sizes, and otherwise makes the same assumptions as those used to develop the estimate of 600,000 homeless persons. The results of changing the assumption about the non-user/user ratio are to reduce the projected size of the national homeless population to approximately 500,000, or 12-17 percent lower than the projections based on a 50/100 ratio. As with all projections, the results are only as good as the assumptions. The reader can adopt any set of reasonable assumptions and work out the projections inherent in them. We believe a reasonable case can be made for both the 50/100 ratio or the 20/100 ratio. With either ratio, the projected population size is one that implies a manageable homeless population toward which programs and services can profitably be directed.

SUMMARY AND IMPLICATIONS

Estimates of the size of the homeless population in many U.S. cities produce rates of homelessness ranging from a high of almost 50/10,000 (in Boston in 1986) to a low of 2.4/10,000 (rural counties in Ohio in 1985). The rate of homelessness is clearly affected by the type of community being examined; roughly, the more densely urban the jurisdiction, the higher the rate of homelessness.

The HUD 1983 estimate of 250,000-350,000 (Department of Housing and Urban Development 1984), the NBER revisions of that estimate of 279,000 for 1983 and of 343,000-363,000 for 1985 (Freeman and Hall 1987), and the ICF re-estimate of 355,000 for 1983 (Committee for Food and Shelter, Inc. 1987) yield results for the entire United States that place the rate of homelessness during the mid-1980s at a figure between 11/10,000 and 15/10,000. Although there has been a good deal of controversy about the original HUD estimate, the very similar estimates developed in the work of these other researchers, who used somewhat varying assumptions and revisions of some of HUD's estimating procedures, lend the HUD estimate considerable credence for the early part of this decade.

Much publicity surrounding homelessness focuses on the extent to which the problem has grown in recent years. The impression that the homeless population has grown rests both on the substantial growth in shelter capacity during the decade and on the sheer visibility of homeless people on the streets of our cities. However, until the Institute's results became available, all projections of the size of the homeless population after 1983 begged the question of population growth, since they started with HUD's 1983 number and applied an arbitrarily selected annual growth rate to the HUD number to create projections for following years.

The new statistical basis provided by the Institute's study means that we can make estimates of the numbers of homeless for 1987 that rely on newly collected data rather than on a projection from HUD's 1983 numbers. These new figures, when compared to estimates for 1983, can begin to answer the question of the growth of the homeless population. The results of this new estimate--a population of approximately 500,000-600,000 people homeless during a seven-day period in March 1987--suggest that the homeless population has indeed grown in the years between 1983 and 1987, to a size approximately double the number of homeless in 1983. The rate of homelessness in 1987, based on the Institute's estimates and projections, lies between 20/10,000 and 25/10,000.

Although this number is significantly lower than most homeless advocates claim, it is still substantial. It implies that more than one million persons in the U.S. were homeless at some time during 1987.[5] If all of these homeless people were gathered together in one place, they would comprise the ninth largest city in the United States. Even the seven-day estimate of 500,000-600,000 produces a homeless population bigger than all but the 25 largest cities in this country. Such a large number of people in this most destitute of conditions strongly suggests that there has been a breakdown in basic systems in this country that are supposed to safeguard the populace from complete impoverishment. Any nation with the wealth of the United States should be able to assure a minimal level of the basic necessities of food and shelter even to its most disabled and disadvantaged citizens. The relatively manageable size of the homeless population means that as a society we could house and maintain the homeless, if we decide to do so.

Notes, chapter 2

1. The homeless rate for Chicago, based on an estimate of the homeless population developed in the 1986 Chicago study, is 7.4/10,000. In contrast, HUD obtained a homeless rate of 66/10,000 based on the provider estimates collected during its 1983 data collection (HUD 1984). The rate of 7.4 seems low when compared to rates in comparable cities, while the rate of 66 seems high.

2. The HUD study director and Westat officials who directed the shelter survey portion of the study indicate that, during debriefing, interviewers were very clear that they had asked about "metropolitan area" and that providers seemed to be responding to "metropolitan area." The shelter universe from which the provider sample was selected also covered the entire metropolitan areas (Deitz 1985).

3. For a complete description of the study's methodology, including the sampling methods used to select cities, providers, and homeless individuals, as well as the weighting methods used to develop estimates of population size, see Burt and Cohen 1988b, volume II, part 2, section B.

4. The confidence interval for the adult estimate is $\pm$ 81,893, or $\pm$ 42 percent of the estimate; the confidence interval for the children's estimate is much smaller ($\pm$ 647, or 1.9 percent).

5. This projection is made as follows: take our estimate, as the number of people homeless in one month; take the number of people who have been homeless for one month or less and multiply by 11 to get the number of people who will become homeless during the remaining 11 months of the year; add the two numbers. This procedure gives an annual incidence that is approximately double the one-month figure.

Chapter Three

THE CHARACTERISTICS AND EATING PATTERNS OF HOMELESS PERSONS WHO USE SOUP KITCHENS AND SHELTERS

Who are the homeless? Until now, the answers to this question have had to rely on data collected from single cities, using a variety of sampling and interviewing methodologies that potentially influenced results as much as the real differences in the homeless population between cities. Only very broad ranges could be established for many variables, often varying by as much as a factor of three or four. For example, the range of "income from working" across twelve studies is 9-37 percent; "high school graduate" ranges from 15-43 percent across ten studies; "families" ranges from 0-35 percent across nine studies.

It is therefore a significant step forward to have developed a national, probability-based sample of homeless adults through the Institute's study. These data provide a strong sense of the average, cross-city values of variables describing the homeless population. They can also help explain some of the differences between cities found with local studies, by contributing to our understanding of the effects of sampling location (that is, shelters, soup kitchens, streets) on who is included in the sample and the probable effects on descriptive statistics of such sample biases. For instance, studies that draw their samples exclusively from shelters are likely to contain higher proportions of individuals who are members of homeless families than are samples drawn exclusively from soup kitchens or from the streets.

Information on homeless persons collected as part of the Institute's 1987 national survey of people who use soup kitchens and shelters is by far the most detailed yet collected on eating patterns of the homeless, and the only nationally representative data set that comes from interviews with the homeless themselves. (See chapter 2 for a description of the sample and sampling methods.) The picture that emerges confirms the findings from other studies limited to single cities, counties, or states. However, the sample is representative of homeless adult users of soup kitchens and shelters in cities of 100,000 population or larger. Therefore, we cannot generalize the data directly to the country as a whole.

A PROFILE OF THE HOMELESS WHO USE SERVICES

Demographic Characteristics

About 229,000 homeless persons in cities with population 100,000 or over used meal or shelter services at some time during a seven-day study period in March 1987. Adults comprise 194,000 of this number; children accompanying these adults make up the remaining 35,000 (see table 3.1).[1]

Most of the homeless adults are male (81 percent in our sample); the majority are nonwhite (54 percent) and between 31 and 50 years of age (51 percent). Homeless persons who use services are three to four times as likely to be black as the general population or the population in metropolitan areas (see table 3.2).[2] They are also slightly more likely to be Hispanic.[3] Almost half (48 percent) have not graduated from high school (see table 3.3), compared to 19 percent of all U.S. adults and 43 percent of all adults below the poverty level in 1986.[4]

Thirty-eight percent of the service-using homeless population use both soup kitchens and shelters; 29 percent use only soup kitchens; the remainder use only shelters

TABLE 3.1 POPULATION SIZE AND SERVICE USE PATTERNS OF
HOMELESS ADULTS AND CHILDREN

| | Homeless individuals who: | | | |
	Only use soup kitchens (N = 223)	Only use shelters (N = 670)	Use both shelters and soup kitchens (N = 811)	Total sample (N = 1,704)
Adults				
1-day estimate				
Number	27,735	42,552	40,047	110,334
Percentage	25	39	36	100
7-day estimate				
Number	57,144	62,552	74,320	194,017
Percentage	29	32	38	100
Children				
1-day estimate				
Number	513	20,799	4,697	26,009
Percentage	1	80	18	100
7-day estimate				
Number	1,790	25,142	7,721	34,653
Percentage	5	73	22	100

"N" refers to unweighted data. The population estimates in this table
are weighted numbers, and the percentages are based on them. See
table 2.3 for confidence intervals.

TABLE 3.2 SEX, RACE, AND AGE OF HOMELESS SERVICE USERS
(weighted percentages)

| Characteristic | Homeless individuals who: | | | |
	Only use soup kitchens (N = 223)	Only use shelters (N = 670)	Use both shelters and soup kitchens (N = 811)	Total sample (N = 1,704)
Total sample	24	36	40	100
Sex				
Male	93	68	84	81
Female	7	32	16	19
	100	100	100	100
Race				
Black	40	35	47	41
White (not Hispanic)	43	51	43	46
Hispanic	13	12	7	10
Other	0	2	3	3
	100	100	100	100
Age				
18-30	20	32	35	30
31-50	65	47	48	51
51-65	11	17	17	16
66+	4	3	0	3
	100	100	100	100

"N" refers to unweighted data. All percentages are based on weighted
data.

TABLE 3.3   HOUSEHOLD COMPOSITION, MARITAL STATUS, AND EDUCATION OF HOME-
LESS SERVICE USERS, BY PATTERN OF SERVICE USE (weighted percentages)

	Homeless individuals who:			
	Only use soup kitchens (N = 223)	Only use shelters (N = 670)	Use both shelters and soup kitchens (N = 811)	Total sample (N = 1,704)
Household Composition				
Single persons	100	100	100	100
Males	83	64	79	75
Females	3	12	6	8
Families (children present)				
Female headed	1	15	5	8
Other (2-parent, or male-headed)	1	3	0	2
Other household types[a]	12	2	1	6
Marital status	100	100	100	100
Currently married	18	7	9	10
Divorced/separated	25	29	32	29
Widowed	3	10	3	5
Never married	55	54	56	55
Education	100	100	100	100
Elementary (0-7)	16	9	5	9
Some high school (8-11)	49	32	40	39
High school graduate	23	31	39	32
Some post high school	8	19	13	14
College graduate	3	9	2	5
Some post college	0	1	1	1

"N" refers to unweighted data. All percentages are based on weighted data.
a. Married or unmarried couples without children; other combinations of relatives without children.

(table 3.1). Those who use only soup kitchens are more likely to be men (93 percent) than the shelter-only group (68 percent) or the group that use both (84 percent). Soup-kitchen-only users are also less likely to be 30 or younger (20 percent) than the shelter-only group (32 percent) or the group that uses both (35 percent). Finally, they are much less likely to be members of families with children present. (Two-thirds of the persons in such families never eat at soup kitchens versus one-third of homeless persons who are not in such families.)

On average, homeless adults tend to be homeless for substantial periods (the median for the whole sample was 10 months, see table 3.4), but such summary figures disguise important differences in patterns of homelessness. One out of five homeless adults (21 percent) have been homeless for three months or less, and half (54 percent) have been homeless for less than one year. At the other extreme, one out of five have been homeless for more than four years. Households with children are much more likely to have been homeless for very short periods of time (41 percent were homeless for three months or less), and only 7 percent experienced homeless episodes of more than four years. In contrast, 21 percent of single men have been homeless for more than four years, and only 17 percent have been homeless for three months or less.

Of all homeless persons, 77 percent are single or unattached adults, 15 percent are children, and 8 percent are the adults in the families to which the children belong. Counting parents with children together as a household, and also counting a single homeless adult as a household, parent-children households make up 10 percent of homeless households. Eighty percent of the parent-child homeless households in our sample are headed by women. Ten percent "families" among the homeless is considerably lower than figures given in recent reports (which range as high as 30 percent). Nevertheless, it is very similar to the 9 percent reported in the only other study of homeless persons that includes a national but non-random sample (derived from individuals who used special health services for the

TABLE 3.4   HISTORY OF HOMELESSNESS AND WORK AMONG
HOMELESS SERVICE USERS, BY PATTERN OF
SERVICE USE (weighted percentages)

| | Homeless individuals who: | | | |
	Use only soup kitchens (N = 223)	Only use shelters (N = 670)	Use both shelters and soup kitchens (N = 811)	Total sample (N = 1,704)
Length of current				
period of homelessness				
< 1 month	5	14	4	8
2-3 months	10	16	12	13
4-6 months	30	16	14	19
7-12 months	7	16	16	14
13-24 months	9	19	17	16
25-48 months	21	8	10	12
> 4 years	18	12	26	19
	100	100	100	100
Mean (in months)	37	33	44	39
Median (in months)	14	7	12	10
Months since				
last steady job				
< 1 month	0	4	1	2
2-3 months	4	12	7	8
4-6 months	12	15	15	14
7-12 months	12	15	19	16
13-24 months	13	16	14	14
25-48 months	13	7	18	13
> 4 years	45	32	26	33
	100	100	100	100
Mean (in months)	67	42	40	48
Median (in months)	26	17	21	21

"N" refers to unweighted data. All percentages are based on weighted data.

homeless in 16 American cities; Wright and Weber 1987).[5] The differences can be attributed at least in part to the presence in both data sets of substantial numbers of homeless persons who do not use shelters, but do frequent soup kitchens and other drop-in services for the homeless. Non-shelter users among homeless adults are very much less likely to have children with them (2 percent) than are homeless individuals who only use shelters (18 percent), and are less than half as likely to have children with them as homeless adults who use both (5 percent) (see table 3.3). Many other attempts to judge the proportion of families among the homeless rely on the estimates of shelter providers. Their judgment may produce inflated estimates for two reasons: first, because they see only the sheltered homeless and not all homeless; and second, because they may count the proportion of the homeless who are family members (including children), rather than the proportion of homeless households that are family households.

Economic Characteristics

The homeless are a very vulnerable group in the population who tend to have both economic and noneconomic problems. Respondents reported very little cash income within the 30 days prior to the interview. The average income per person for the preceding 30 days was $137, which is 28 percent of the federal poverty level for a one-person household in 1987.[6] Seventeen percent reported no cash income during this period. Homeless persons who used only soup kitchens had substantially lower mean incomes ($94/month) than users of shelters (about $150/month). They also had less education and had been homeless and jobless longer. Men were more likely to report income from handouts or from working, women from means-tested benefits (see table 3.5).

The homeless in our sample had also typically been without a job for a considerable period of time--about four years on average, with a median of 20 months (see table 3.4). These homeless adults had been jobless for a good deal longer than they had been homeless. About half of single

TABLE 3.5   CURRENT SOURCES OF INCOME AMONG HOMELESS SERVICE-USERS, BY SELECTED CHARACTERISTICS (weighted percentages; N = 1,704)

	Working	AFDC	GA	SSI	Food stamps	Other benefits[a]	Hand-outs	Other[b]
					Percentage who received income from:			
Total sample	25	5	12	4	18	7	17	31
Sex								
Male	25	2	9	3	13	7	18	43
Female	18	17	28	8	37	6	9	32
Race								
Black	19	7	16	3	20	6	15	34
White	28	2	7	5	14	9	15	50
Hispanic	30	7	20	3	23	4	17	32
Age								
≤ 30	33	9	15	2	18	3	21	46
31-50	25	4	11	4	18	4	17	46
51-65	9	1	14	5	19	17	10	24
66+	12	0	0	19	3	65	1	2
Homeless with child								
Yes	23	33	33	2	48	4	4	26
No	24	1	10	4	14	7	18	43
Education								
Less than 12 years	22	5	12	4	16	7	20	39
12 years or more	26	4	12	3	19	7	16	45

"N" refers to unweighted data. All percentages are based on weighted data.
a. SSDI, Social Security, veteran's benefits, workers' compensation, unemployment insurance.
b. Received money from relatives, friends, trading or swapping things, gifts, selling blood, other.

homeless men and half of homeless women with children had not held a steady job (defined as three months or longer with the same employer) in more than two years. Only about one in ten homeless adults had held a regular job within the three months prior to the interview. Coupled with information about the generally low receipt of public benefits by respondents, these data support an interpretation that economic problems contributed to becoming homeless.

Researchers have not been able to generalize the findings of earlier studies of the homeless in different cities. Potential major differences in the homeless populations of the cities studied and the sometimes profound effects that different sampling methods and sources of respondents may have on results have produced widely varying estimates of basic characteristics of the homeless. The Institute's study provides the first opportunity to examine cross-city data on the underlying central tendencies of critical descriptive characteristics. Table 3.6 summarizes the Institute's results for key demographic and economic variables (first column) and displays comparable statistics from fourteen local studies that interviewed homeless individuals.

On most variables in table 3.6 (sex, race, age, marital status, education, receipt of income maintenance, and work experience), the Institute's figures lie squarely in the middle of the range of estimates produced by the local studies. These results suggest that the true value of any variable describing the national homeless population is likely to lie somewhere in the middle of the range of values derived from local estimates. However, the breadth of some of the ranges (for example, from 23 percent to 74 percent non-white) also implies strong local variations on key variables that could push local policies toward the homeless in different directions.

Only for length of homelessness do the Institute's data lie on the extreme. Although lack of consistency in reporting data on length of homelessness across studies makes comparison difficult, it still appears that the Institute's sample has fewer short-term homeless and more long-term homeless than do other studies. It may be that the

TABLE 3.6   COMPARISONS OF DESCRIPTIVE DATA ON THE HOMELESS FROM OTHER STUDIES

	Urban Institute (1987)	3 California counties (1988)	Seattle (1986)	Cincin-nati (1986)	Chicago (1985-86)
Sex -- % Male	81	73	52	65	76
Race -- % Non-white	54	47	49	39	69
Age					
% ≤ 30	30	62[a]	49[b]	29	25
% 31-50	51	32[c]	23[d]	27[e]	55[c]
Marital status					
% never married	55	49	n.a.	n.a.	57
Education					
% high school graduate or more	52	n.a.	n.a.	n.a.	55
Length of time homeless					
≤ 3 months	21	n.a.	n.a.	n.a.	32
> 12 months	47	n.a.	n.a.	13	39
> 4 years	19	n.a.	n.a.	n.a.	13
Income maintenance[k]					
% yes, now	20	28	n.a.	24	35
Worked for pay last month -- % yes	25	n.a.	n.a.	n.a.	39
Respondendents from					
Soup kitchen	X	--	--	--	--
Shelter	X	X	X	X	X
Street	--	X	--	--	X
N =	1,704	315	351	801	722

Note: a. 17-34   c. 31-54   e. 31-45
         b. 18-44   d. 45-59   k. AFDC, GA or SSI

TABLE 3.6   (Continued)

	Minne-apolis (1985-86)	Massa-chustts (1985)	Multnomah County, OR (1985)	L.A. DMH (1984-85)	L.A. UCLA (1984-85)
Sex -- % Male	85	81	0	96	77
Race -- % Non-white	54	30	27	73	49
Age					
% ≤ 30	63[a]	48[a]	67[a]	36	n.a.
% 31-50	37[f]	38[f]	29[f]	45	n.a.
Marital status					
% never married	53	61	29	59	55
Education					
% high school graduate or more	47	52	52	51	65
Length of time homeless					
≤ 3 months	n.a.	n.a.	33	55[g]	43
> 12 months	n.a.	n.a.	41	30	36
> 4 years	n.a.	n.a.	n.a.	n.a.	8[i]
Income maintenance[k]					
% yes, now	n.a.	37	19	15	25
Worked for pay last month -- % yes	36	25	n.a.	32	19
Respondendents from					
Soup kitchen	X	--	X	X	X
Shelter	X	X	X	X	X
Street	X	X	X	X	--
N =	339	282	190	379	266

Note: a. 17-34   i. ≥ 5 years
        f. 35-54   k. AFDC, GA or SSI
        g. ≤ 6 months

TABLE 3.6   (Continued)

	Detroit (1984-85)	Milwaukee (1984-85)	Ohio (1984)	Maltnomah County, OR (1984)	Chicago (1985-86)
Sex -- % Male	71	87	81	85	67
Race -- % Non-white	74	40	33	23	59
Age					
% $\leq$ 30	(X=	31	35	29	43[a]
% 31-50	35)	47	44	48	49[c]
Marital status					
% never married	52	36	45	40	n.a.
Education					
% high school graduate or more	43	n.a.	44	47	n.a.
Length of time homeless					
$\leq$ months	n.a.	32[h]	49[h]	33	37[h]
> 12 months	n.a.	28	27	41	28
> 4 years	n.a.	8[j]	n.a.	n.a.	16[j]
Income maintenance[k]					
% yes, now	n.a.	32	24	13	22
Worked for pay last month -- % yes	12	n.a.	25	18	n.a.
Respondendents from					
Soup kitchen	--	--	X	X	--
Shelter	X	X	X	X	--
Street	--	X	X	X	X
N =	75	237	979	131	80

Note: a. 17-34   h. $\leq$ 2 months
        c. 31-54   k. AFDC, GA or SSI
        j. $\geq$ 3 years

frequency-of-use adjustment employed in the Institute's weighting procedures, which gave more weight to infrequent service users (who also tended to be the longer-term homeless), produced this result. The inclusion in our samples of the homeless soup kitchen users who do not use shelters probably also contributed to this difference.

Physical and Mental Health Problems

The homeless who use soup kitchens and shelters tend to be in relatively poor physical and mental health. A majority (56 percent) reported at least one health problem, including 15 percent with joint problems, 15 percent with high blood pressure, and 10 percent with problems walking (see table 3.7). Their self-reported health status was also low. Thirty-eight percent said their health was fair or poor, compared with 10 percent of the general population ages 18-64 and 20 percent of the low-income population ages 4-86+.[7] Data from Wright and Weber's very extensive study of health conditions among the homeless, strongly supports the impression from our limited data that the homeless suffer from comparatively poor health. In fact, Wright and Weber report that physical health problems are important contributors to *becoming* homeless, in addition to the health problems that arise as a *consequence* of homelessness.

Mental health problems also were relatively prevalent in the sample. Nineteen out of 100 reported a history of mental hospitalization. Among those who have such a history, almost half (46 percent) also have experienced at least one institutionalization for chemical dependency, which for most homeless people probably occurred in a detoxification center. A similar proportion (19 percent) reported having tried to commit suicide (versus 3 out of 100 for the general population and 7 out of 100 for persons ever diagnosed as suffering from a major psychiatric diagnosis).[8]

Different subgroups among the homeless vary substantially in their reporting of mental health indicators (see table 3.8). Homeless single women are most likely to report both mental hospitalization and at least one suicide

TABLE 3.7   PERCEPTIONS OF HEALTH AND REPORTED
            HEALTH PROBLEMS (weighted percentages);
            N = 1,704

Number of health problems reported	
None	44
1 problem	31
2 problems	11
3 problems	8
4 or more problems	7
	100

Types of health problems reported	
None	44
Upper respiratory tract infections (colds, coughs, bronchitis)	21
Arthritis, rheumatism, joint problems	15
High blood pressure	15
Problems walking, lost limb, etc.	10
Heart disease/stroke	8
Problems with the liver, jaundice	8
Anemia (poor blood)	6
Diabetes (sugar in the blood)	4
Pneumonia	4
Tuberculosis	2
Other health problems	19

Perceptions of health status	Urban Institute national	NCHS-national	
		All	Low-income
Excellent	14	38	28
Very good	17	29	23
Good	35	24	28
Fair	25	7	20
Poor	13	3	
	100	100	100

"N" refers to unweighted data. All percentages are based on weighted data.

TABLE 3.8   PERSONAL PROBLEMS (weighted percentages)

	Single women (N=278)	Women w/ children (N=268)	Single men (N=140)
History of:			
Mental hospitalization	24	8	20
Inpatient chemical Dependency treatment	19	7	37
Neither	64	89	53
Either, but not both	29	8	38
Both	7	3	10
History of time served in:			
Jail for 5+ days	22	15	60
State or federal prison	2	2	29
Neither	78	85	35
Either, but not both	20	13	40
Both	2	2	25
Percent with no institutional history	55	80	26
Percent with history in 3 or all 4 types of institutions[a]	5	3	21
Other mental illness indicators			
Percentage ever attempted suicide	24	14	21
Percentage above CES-D clinical cutoff[b]	45	41	52
Mean CES-D score	15	17	17

"N" refers to unweighted data. All percentages are based on weighted data. Percentages may not sum to 100 due to rounding.
a. Mental hospitalization, chemical dependency inpatient treatment, jail, prison.
b. CES-D Scale developed by NIMH Center for Epidemiological Studies to measure depression. A short (six item) version was used in this study.

attempt (24 percent for each); homeless single men are close behind, with 20 percent reporting hospitalization and 21 percent reporting suicidal behavior. The homeless women who have children with them stand out as the exceptions; only 8 percent report mental hospitalizations. However, 14 percent report suicidal behavior which, while considerably lower than such attempts among the single homeless of either sex, is still about five times the rate for the general adult population.

Finally, on a scale measuring current depression and demoralization, 49 percent of the homeless had high enough psychological distress to indicate the need for immediate treatment.[9] Items on this scale include:

✦ Was your appetite so poor that you did not feel like eating?
✦ Did you feel so tired and worn out that you could not enjoy anything?
✦ Did you feel depressed?
✦ Did you feel unhappy about the way your life was going?
✦ Did you feel discouraged and worried about your future?
✦ Did you feel lonely?

With this item content, it is perhaps not so surprising that one in every two homeless persons registered on the scale as highly distressed. Given the strains caused by homelessness, the wonder is that the proportion was no higher.

Institutionalization

Institutionalization for alcohol, drug abuse, or crime is also prevalent. One-third of the respondents had been patients in a detoxification or alcohol/drug treatment center. Of these, one in four had also been hospitalized for mental illness. In fact, 21 percent of respondents who reported at least one of these types of institutionalization (mental illness or chemical dependency) also reported the other, and fully 43 percent of homeless adults have experienced at least one.

Evidence of criminal justice involvement is also high. Sixty percent of the single men, 22 percent of the single women, and 15 percent of the women with children had spent more than three or four days in a county jail. Although we have no evidence directly from our survey, other reports on the homeless suggest that some of this time in jail may be a direct consequence of being homeless. Additionally, 29 percent of single men reported having served time in a state or federal prison (presumably for a felony). The state or federal imprisonment rate for women, whether single or with children, is much lower, at 2 percent.

Two-thirds of all respondents had experienced at least one of the four types of institutionalization included in the interview (detoxification or other chemical dependency inpatient treatment, jail, prison, mental hospital). About one-quarter had experienced only one type, but 18 percent had been institutionalized in three or in all four of the four types of institutions. These proportions again vary greatly depending on whether one considers single men, single women, or women with children. Women with children have the lowest probability of institutionalization; only one in five has been in any of these institutions. At the opposite extreme, three of every four single men have been in at least one institution.

These data paint a picture of a homeless population in which many individuals have a significant number of serious disabilities. Their disabilities probably contributed to their becoming homeless. For instance, Wright and Weber (1987) place three health-related disabilities--mental illness, chemical dependency and physical health problems--among the top ten factors rated by medical practitioners as contributing to the loss of housing for patients of the Robert Wood Johnson Foundation Health Care for the Homeless projects in 13 cities. These same disabilities also affect the ease or difficulty of helping currently homeless people to achieve and maintain permanent housing. At the very least, the extent of serious health disabilities suggests that housing solutions must include not simply financial assistance or public housing, but also supportive services that can help the disabled deal with the life crises that can destabilize them and ultimately result in a return to the streets.

EATING PATTERNS

Unique among studies of the homeless, the Institute's survey collected data on the food sources and eating patterns of homeless individuals. Relatively few local studies included any questions on either of these topics, and rarely were questions similar enough to compare findings across studies. Nevertheless, food and shelter are equally basic, and equally important to the homeless--shelter might be more critical to survival on a freezing night but, on a daily basis, many homeless people go without shelter who cannot go without food. Policymakers should find this new information of great interest.

As will be seen in chapter 4, the meals available to homeless people through soup kitchens and shelters are of relatively good variety and nutrient content. The data available from individuals do not allow us to determine where people ate all of their meals. We do know from provider data collected by the Institute that 321,000 provider meals are available each day in cities of 100,000 or more, and we estimate there are 229,000 homeless persons, including children, in these cities. These figures would suggest that only 1.4 provider meals are available for each homeless person every day. Since homeless individuals may eat less adequate meals elsewhere, we can draw no firm conclusions about the nutritional quality of their total diet. However, the Institute's data on homeless individuals' eating patterns suggest that their diet is less than adequate on a number of dimensions--frequency and regularity of eating, quality of food, and variety of foods eaten that might supply a range of needed nutrients as well as calories.

It will come as no surprise to most readers to learn that homeless people do not eat well. Our results depict the nature and extent of deficiencies in their eating patterns (see table 3.9). Most homeless people, for example, do not eat three meals a day, as does the average American. Three out of four homeless people eat two meals a day or less; 63 percent eat two or more meals a day; and only 25 percent average three or more meals. Shelter users are much more likely to be among this more fortunate group, while among those who rely solely on soup kitchens, only about one in ten eat three or more meals a day. The average number of meals eaten daily was 1.9, compared to three or more meals a day for the average American.

Homeless people also go whole days without food. Thirty-six percent reported that they go one day or more *per week* without eating anything; when interviewers asked homeless individuals to describe what they ate during the 24 hours before the interview, about one in twelve said they had eaten nothing. One in six said they go two days or more without eating as often as once a week; one in eight said they go two days or more without eating once or twice month. These patterns of deprivation are most likely to characterize single men among the homeless, with 40 percent going at least one day out of seven without eating anything compared to slightly under 20 percent for both single women and women with children.

Not only do these homeless people eat relatively infrequently, they eat relatively little. The median number of servings of all foods consumed by homeless people on the day before the interview ranged between 6 for individuals who only used soup kitchens, to 10 for individuals who used only shelters. The median for the entire sample was 9 servings of all foods (see table 3.10). This compares to a USDA recommendation of 15-25 servings per day just of foods in the five essential food groups, not counting the miscellaneous servings that most people eat of sweets, baked goods, or salty snacks (Human Nutrition Information Service 1986). Thus homeless adults in this study ate, on average, only about half the quantity of food recommended daily by the USDA.

TABLE 3.9 REPORTED FREQUENCY OF EATING AMONG HOME-
LESS SERVICE USERS, BY PATTERN OF SERVICE USE
(weighted percentages)

| | Homeless individuals who: | | | |
Question	Only use soup kitchens (N = 223)	Only use shelters (N = 670)	Use both shelters and soup kitchens (N = 811)	Total sample (N = 1,704)
"How many times do you usually eat in a day?"				
Less than once	21	1	3	7
Once	27	23	37	30
Twice	40	36	39	38
Three times	8	31	18	20
Four times	2	8	2	4
> four times	2	1	1	1
	100	100	100	100
"During the last seven days, did you go a whole day without eating? How often?"				
None	41	77	68	64
One	40	14	12	19
Two	13	4	10	9
Three	5	1	8	5
Four or more	1	4	2	3
	100	100	100	100
"Ever go without anything to eat for two or more days at a time? How often?"				
Never	51	72	62	63
Few times a year	10	7	8	8
Once a month	3	5	9	6
Twice a month	9	4	6	6
Once a week	27	12	15	17
	100	100	100	100

"N" refers to unweighted data. All percentages are based on weighted data.

TABLE 3.10   ABSENCE FROM DIET OF SPECIFIC FOOD GROUPS AMONG HOMELESS SERVICE USERS (weighted percentages)

Type of food absent	Homeless individuals who:			
	Only use soup kitchens (N = 223)	Only use shelters (N = 670)	Use both shelters and soup kitchens (N = 811)	Total sample (N = 1,704)
No consumption of food group during previous day				
Grain products	44	23	25	30
Meat/meat alternates	19	17	24	20
Fruits/vegetables	45	41	43	43
Milk/milk products	67	61	67	65
Miscellaneous foods	50	31	31	36
No consumption of any food	8	11	4	8
Median number of servings of all foods	6	10	8	9

"N" refers to unweighted data. All percentages are based on weighted data.

The diets of homeless people also suffer in quality--they lack certain essential foods. The U.S. Department of Agriculture states that daily consumption of foods from five food groups (milk and milk products, grain products, fruits, vegetables, and meat and meat alternates) is essential for healthy nutrition (Human Nutrition Information Service 1986). Our data show that, on average, each day homeless people eat foods from only 2.7 of these five essential food groups. Descriptions of what homeless people said they ate the day before the interview indicate that 65 percent had not consumed any milk or milk products during that day, 43 percent had eaten no fruits or vegetables, 30 percent had eaten no grain products, and 20 percent had eaten no meat or meat alternates such as dry beans, peas, and peanut butter (see table 3.10). A survey of national eating patterns over a one-day period, the Nationwide Food Consumption Survey 1977-78, found that 19 percent of Americans had eaten no milk or milk products, 14 percent had eaten no vegetables, 46 percent had eaten no fruits, 4 percent had eaten no grain products, and 7 percent had eaten no meat or meat alternates (Human Nutrition Information Service 1980). Obviously the diet of the average American is consistently more adequate than that of the average homeless person, with the possible exception of fruit consumption.

Consistent with these estimates, a majority of homeless individuals in this study perceived the healthfulness of their diets as only fair (28 percent) or poor (23 percent). Only 18 percent said their diets were excellent or very good. Thirty-eight percent reported that they sometimes or often did not get enough to eat, compared with 4 percent of all U.S. households and 20 percent of all U.S. households with incomes below 76 percent of the official poverty line (Mathematica Policy Research 1987).

Those who used only soup kitchens but never went to shelters ate less well than those who used shelters as well or shelters only. Soup-kitchen-only users reported fewer meals per day, more days in the week without eating, more periods of going two days or more without eating, and poorer outcomes on other indicators of eating patterns. The more outcomes on other indicators of eating patterns. The more often homeless people ate at a shelter during the week, the better their diet and eating patterns.

HOW INDIVIDUALS COMPARE WITH FAMILIES AMONG THE SERVICE-USING HOMELESS POPULATION

According to our estimate, 10 percent of homeless households are families with children present. As indicated earlier, 8 percent of the homeless are adults in families with children and 15 percent are children in those families. Considering only the adults, approximately 138,000, or 79 percent, of our estimated 194,000 homeless adults who used soup kitchens and shelters in large U.S. cities in March 1987, were single men. Approximately 18,000 (10 percent) were single women and 16,000 were women accompanied by at least one child (9 percent). The remainder, about 2,000 or 1 percent, were men with children. Thus approximately half of homeless adult women have children with them and are counted as family households in our analysis, compared to virtually none of the men. Homeless adults who have children with them are substantially different from other homeless persons.[10]

The finding that only 10 percent of the households in our sample are family households (defined as at least one adult who is homeless with at least one child) is substantially lower than estimates of many other studies. There are three major reasons for this difference: (1) our figure of 10 percent is a count of households, not of individuals; (2) our sample contains people who do not use shelters but do use soup kitchens; and, (3) we used a frequency-of-use adjustment in weighting the sample. Table 3.11 shows the effects of each of these factors.

In each panel of table 3.11, the first row shows the percentage of all households that are family households (adult[s] plus at least one child). For this analysis, each

TABLE 3.11   THE EFFECTS OF DIFFERENT WAYS OF COUNTING
HOMELESS FAMILIES (weighted percentages)

| | Homeless individuals who: | | Total sample (N=1,704) |
	Use soup kitchens but not shelters[a] (N=223)	Use shelters[b] (N=1,481)	
1-day estimate			
Family households as percentage of all households	1	17	13
Family members as percentage of all individuals	3	37	30
Adults	1	13	10
Children	2	24	20
7-day estimate			
Family households as percentage of all households	2	13	10
Family members as percentage of all individuals	5	28	23
Adults	2	8	8
Children	3	20	15

"N" refers to unweighted data of interview respondents, all of whom were
adults. Estimates of the numbers and proportions of children are based
on the adult respondents' reports of how many children were homeless
with them. All percentages are based on weighted data.
a. Everyone in this category is homeless; sampling methods screened out
people in soup kitchens who were not homeless.
b. This category includes individuals who use both shelters and soup
kitchens, and those who only use shelters.

unattached homeless person counts as a one-person household. The second row shows the percentage of all homeless individuals, including children, who are members of homeless families. It is easy to see by comparing these two rows in each panel that the proportion of households that are families is considerably smaller than the proportion of individuals who are family members.

A comparison of the first with the second column in table 3.11 clearly demonstrates that homeless people who use only soup kitchens are much less likely to be family households or family members than the homeless who use shelters. Any study that relies exclusively on a shelter-based homeless population is going to overestimate the proportion of families and family members among the homeless.

Finally, comparing the two panels in table 3.11 reveals the substantial difference created by different weighting schemes. The seven-day weights are used to create all figures reported in this volume except where explicitly stated otherwise. The seven-day weights have been adjusted for frequency of use. A person who used a shelter or soup kitchen on all seven of the days prior to the interview would have an adjustment weight of one, and would count only for him or herself. A person who used a shelter or soup kitchen only once during the same seven days would have an adjustment weight of seven--he or she would be counted as representing six other people with similar characteristics and service use patterns. This adjustment is based on the assumption that soup kitchens and shelters serve approximately the same number of people per day on the days they are open, and that infrequent users are replaced by others like themselves on days that they do not use a service.

Since family households tend to be much more constant users of services than singles, singles receive higher weights in this frequency-of-use adjustment. In consequence, the adjustment produces estimates of higher proportions of single individuals/households, and lower proportions of family members and family households. We maintain that the seven-day weights are a more accurate reflection of the true numbers of people who are homeless during a given week than the one-day weights, and therefore have used seven-day weights throughout this report. However, we present the one-day-weight results for the families because they help to resolve the issue of why our estimates of families and family members are so much lower than those in many other published reports. In table 3.11 the proportion of shelter-using family members obtained using the one-day weight is the closest conceptually to other reports and yields the closest results.

The vast majority of adults with children present were female (88 percent). Exactly the reverse sex ratio was held among the homeless by themselves (88 percent male). Adults with children present were also more likely to be black (54 versus 39 percent) or Hispanic (20 versus 9 percent) than were the homeless living alone. About half of both groups had never been married; but the adults with children present were more likely to be currently married (23 versus 9 percent). Those homeless by themselves were more likely to have lived prior to homelessness in a single room or some kind of institution (mental hospital, jail, halfway house, detox center, etc.) than were adults with children present (31 versus 8 percent).

Homeless families had been homeless for substantially less time than single homeless persons (the median was 4.5 months versus 12 months). However, neither the adults in homeless families nor the single homeless had much of a history of steady work. Both had been without work for about four years on average, with a median of 20 months.

Adults in homeless families were more likely to be current recipients of public benefits (AFDC: families 33 percent; alone 1 percent; General Assistance (GA): families 33 percent, alone 10 percent). They also received more cash income last month as a result of benefit receipt (median household income was $300 versus $64 for the single homeless). However, family households, with an average of three persons, had to spread their $300 over more people, producing a median per person income of about $100. While still higher than the median income of single homeless adults, $100 per person, per month is not adequate to cover the cost of living in most localities.

More homeless families than single homeless persons receive food stamps (50 percent versus 15 percent). The average monthly benefit level *per person* is higher for single people than for family households ($59 versus $35 per person). This difference arises because there are more people in family households and the benefit levels for additional people are lower than for the first person.

Adults homeless by themselves were more likely to report that their diet was fair or poor (52 versus 44 percent for homeless families), and less likely to report that it was excellent, very good, or good than homeless adults in families. Single homeless were also somewhat more likely to say that they sometimes or often did not get enough to eat (39 versus 29 percent for homeless families).

These perceptions are corroborated by data on reported frequency of eating and dietary content. More homeless by themselves reported eating two or fewer times a day (77 percent) than adults in homeless families (59 percent). Single homeless persons were also more likely to have gone one or more days without eating during the last seven days (38 versus 16 percent), and to report occasions on which they went two or more days without eating (39 versus 21 percent).

Adults in homeless families reported eating somewhat less food than single homeless adults--as measured by the number of servings of all foods they consumed on the day before the interview (8.5 servings for adults in families versus 9.1 for single adults). But single homeless persons consumed foods from fewer of the five essential food groups: the mean number of groups was 2.6, versus 2.9 for adults in families (and 2.7 for the entire sample).

The typical diet for adults in families, however, compares poorly to that of to the average American. Nine servings of all foods is significantly less than the USDA recommendations of 15-25 servings of foods from the five essential food groups per day. And the mean number of 2.6 to 2.9 essential food groups included in the diets of homeless adults is also significantly fewer than USDA recommendations to eat foods from all five essential food groups every day for good health.

Adults in homeless families report less satisfaction with their diet, eat fewer meals each day, and are more likely to go whole days without food than the average American. Only 37 percent of adults in families and 27 percent of single adults consumed foods from four or from all five of the essential food groups on the day preceding the interview. In comparison, the daily diets of most American adults contain foods from four or all five essential food groups.

Adults in homeless families were much more likely than singles to have spent all of the past week in a shelter (66 versus 31 percent) and much less likely to have avoided shelters altogether during the week (4 versus 27 percent). They also were much less likely to have eaten in soup kitchens; 69 versus 32 percent did not eat any meals in soup kitchens during the week before the interview. Since shelters that provide food serve more meals a day, and on more days a week than soup kitchens, families in food-providing shelters benefit from this pattern. Single adults and adults in families who use shelters were about equally likely to have eaten meals prepared by the shelter where they lived. Many of the families may have made their own meals at their shelter, however, especially if it was a battered women's shelter, a family shelter with kitchen facilities, or a welfare hotel.

Finally, single homeless adults had much more troubled histories than adults in homeless families (see the comparison of women with children to single males and females in table 3.6). They were more likely to have experienced both mental hospitalization and inpatient treatment for alcohol or drug dependency. They were much more likely to have spent time in jail and in a state or federal prison. And they were much more likely to have experienced more than one of these types of trouble. Only 12 percent of the adults in families had experienced two or more types of trouble, for example, compared with 42 percent of single homeless persons. The pattern for current depression/

demoralization is different however. Adults with children present had as high scores on this scale as homeless alone--an indication that being homeless is an extremely difficult circumstance to cope with, irrespective of one's general mental or psychological health.

As noted earlier, we did not directly interview homeless children. The data on the adults with whom they live, however, suggest that they may be homeless for shorter periods than the average homeless person, they may eat somewhat better, and the adults who care for them may be less emotionally disturbed.

We also examined the impact of demographic characteristics, benefits receipt, and other factors on eating frequency (number of times the respondent eats daily, number of days during the previous week the respondent did not eat anything) and diet quality (number of servings of all foods and number of five essential food groups represented in the diet of respondents on the day before the interview). On first examining these issues, it became apparent that our expectations for the impact of several important predictor variables were contingent on a respondent's household status: single or homeless with children. Therefore we ran regressions separately for these two subgroups among the homeless (see tables 3.12 and 3.13).

These analyses reveal quite different patterns of significance for single homeless and adults with children. The resource variables (receiving income maintenance now, per person value of food stamps received, number of days of the previous week that respondent received meals prepared at a shelter) affect the quality and quantity of food intake for the singles but not for the adults with children. This difference may occur because family households are more consistently sheltered than singles, and either receive meals prepared by their shelter or have facilities available where they can cook. Indeed, having a place to cook food does affect the diet quality of homeless households with children but not of the single homeless. Adult homeless with children appear actually to eat less well when they must prepare their own food for themselves and their children under shelter

TABLE 3.12   FACTORS ASSOCIATED WITH FREQUENCY OF
EATING AMONG HOMELESS SERVICE USERS
(standardized regression coefficients); N = 1,704

| | Dependent variable: | | | |
| | Daily[a] | | Days without Eating[b] | |
Independent variables	Singles	Families	Singles	Families
Receives income maintenance now	-.040	.254	-.158+	-.017
Food stamp benefit received - $ per person/month (range=$0-$81)	.193*	.121	-.056	.024
Reported income/last 30 days	.054	-.189	.014	-.008
Has a place to cook food	-.036	-.036	-.032	-.081
Age	.014	-.310*	.105	.007
Education	.179*	-.245*	-.215**	.166*
Minority status (1=yes; 0=no)	.045	.112	.013	-.067
Gender (1=female 0=male)	-.175**	-.106	-.058	-.757***
Mental hospitalization (1=yes; 0=no)	.083	-.090	.034	.002
Drug/alcohol treatment (1=yes; 0=no)	-.109	-.273+	.274***	.110
Current depression/demoralization (CES-D - high = more)	-.113+	.026	.182*	.019
Months since last steady job	.043	-.112	.060	-.020
Months of homelessness	.114	-.001	-.156+	.138*
Days/week eat at shelter	.197**	.083	-.074	-.085
Number of servings of alcohol	.027	-.018	-.031	-.202**
Reported number of health problems	-.223**	-.218+	-.253**	.109
Adjusted R^2	.299	.235	.143	.663

"N" refers to unweighted data. Regressions are based on weighted data.

a. "Daily" = number of times the respondent eats daily; higher = more often.
b. Number of days without eating during past week; higher = more often.

+ $p < .10$;   * $p < .05$;   ** $p < .01$;   *** $p < .001$

TABLE 3.13   EFFECT OF VARIOUS FACTORS ON QUANTITY AND QUALITY OF FOOD CONSUMED BY SINGLE HOMELESS AND MEMBERS OF HOMELESS FAMILIES (standardized regression coefficients; N = 1,704)

| | Dependent variable: | | | |
| | Number of servings (0-68) | | Number of five essential food groups (0-5) | |
Independent variables Range =	Singles	Families	Singles	Families
Receives income maintenance now	.217**	.088	.136+	.110
Food stamp benefit received - $ per person/month (range=$0-$81)	.134+	.142	.140+	.173
Reported income/last 30 days	-.063	.063	-.082	.042
Has a place to cook food	-.093	-.271**	-.051	-.200*
Age	-.156+	-.133	-.038	.074
Education	-.012	-.188+	.047	-.267*
Minority status (1=yes; 0=no)	-.213**	.224+	-.148*	.096
Gender (1=female 0=male)	.121+	.101	.106+	-.107
Mental hospitalization (1=yes; 0=no)	-.142+	.231*	-.191**	.198+
Drug/alcohol treatment (1=yes; 0=no)	.015	.173	-.114+	-.064
Current depression/demoralization (CES-D - high = more)	-.002	-.170	-.016	.007
Months since last steady job	.198**	-.216+	.229***	-.350**
Months of homelessness	.150+	-.276**	.264***	-.255*
Days/week eat at shelter	.245**	.028	.284***	-.138
Number of servings of alcohol	-.022	.078	.111+	.050
Reported number of health problems	-.105	.123	-.131	-.024
Adjusted R²	.223	.354	.342	.224

"N" refers to unweighted data. Regressions are based on weighted data.

   + p < .10;   * p < .05;   ** p < .01;   *** p < .001

conditions. This would suggest that having a place to cook food is the most important factor in the analysis for adults with children, whereas the other resource factors have more effect for the singles, very few of whom have access to cooking facilities.

Several health and mental health conditions also affect eating frequency and diet adequacy. For singles, a history of mental hospitalization, inpatient chemical dependency treatment, and high scores on current depression/ demoralization have a negative effect. Also, the higher the number of reported physical health problems, the less frequently both singles and adults with children eat during an average day. However, for singles, health problems are also associated with fewer days of the week on which the respondent goes without eating entirely. Finally, several variables appear to affect singles and adults with children in opposite ways. More education and longer periods of homelessness and joblessness are associated with better eating patterns for singles but worse eating patterns for adults with children. Minority status and a history of mental hospitalization show the reverse pattern. The reasons for these opposite effects are unclear. Before developing potential explanations, it is probably worth seeing whether any other studies replicate these results.

THE HOMELESS WHO DO NOT USE SERVICES

The Urban Institute's study focused on homeless adults who use soup kitchens and shelters--because these facilities form the base of a feasible sampling methodology using probability methods. However, it was also important to determine whether the homeless who do use services differ in important ways from those who do not, and also whether those who use services benefit from them in ways that non-service users cannot match with other resources. The results of this analysis have implications for the importance of outreach programs to contact non-service users in order to encourage them to take advantage of the services available, and for attempts to find ways to restructure services to make them easier to use.

To gather data on the homeless who do not use services for comparison purposes, we interviewed homeless persons at congregating sites (such as bus stations and parks) who had not used any kind of shelter or soup kitchen for the past week. Of the 445 people identified as homeless at these sites, only 32 percent, or 142 people, had *not* used a soup kitchen or a shelter during the past week. We cannot make rigorous statistical comparisons between the service-using homeless and this small and not necessarily representative sample of non-service users. Nevertheless, the general picture is relatively clear (see tables 3.14, 3.15 and 3.16).

A whole variety of comparisons indicates that the homeless who do not use services fare less well than those who do. The homeless who do not use services reported being homeless longer, having been without a steady job for longer and having made less use of public benefits. They also reported being less healthy and having more mental problems.

The homeless who do not use services also had poorer eating patterns than the service-using homeless on every measure. They relied much more heavily on trash and on handouts as sources of food. They ate fewer meals per day, averaging only one meal per day (mean = 1.36) compared to the almost two meals of the service users (mean = 1.92). They were much more likely to have gone one or more days without eating during the seven days prior to the interview, with a mean of somewhat over one day (1.35) in comparison to a mean of under one day for service users (0.66).

The homeless who do not use services were less likely to report getting enough to eat, and were quite unlikely to get what they wanted to eat. More nonusers than users described the quality of their diet as fair or poor, and were less likely to have eaten foods from the five essential food groups.

TABLE 3.14   COMPARISON OF DEMOGRAPHIC AND
OTHER CHARACTERISTICS OF HOMELESS
PEOPLE WHO DO AND DO NOT USE
SERVICES   (percentages)

Characteristic	Non-users (N=142)[a]	Users (N=1,704)[b]
Sex: percentage male	89	81
Race:		
black	54	41
white (not hispanic)	34	46
hispanic	9	10
other	3	3
	100	100
Age:		
18-30	21	30
31-50	55	51
51-65	21	16
> 65	3	3
	100	100
Marital status: percentage never married	49	55
Education: percentage high school graduate	45	52

a. No weight possible for nonusers. Percentages based on
unweighted data.

b. Percentages based on weighted data, as the best
estimate for service users.

TABLE 3.14   (Continued)

Characteristic	Non-users (N=142)[a]	Users (N=1,704)[b]
Length of time homeless:		
< 1 month	5	8
2-3 months	9	13
4-6 months	8	19
7-12 months	16	14
13-24 months	15	16
25-48 months	17	12
> 48 months	31	19
	100	100
Length of time since last steady job:		
< 1 month	1	2
2-3 months	5	8
4-6 months	5	14
7-12 months	15	16
13-24 months	14	14
25-48 months	20	13
> 48 months	40	33
	100	100
Percentage receiving income maintenance:	9	20
Food stamp receipt:		
% now	9	18
% before	32	41
% never	59	41

a. No weight possible for nonusers. Percentages based on unweighted data.
b. Percentages based on weighted data, as the best estimate for service users.

TABLE 3.15 COMPARISON OF HEALTH, MENTAL HEALTH, AND
INSTITUTIONALIZATIONS AMONG HOMELESS PEOPLE
WHO DO AND DO NOT USE SERVICES (percentages)

Characteristic	Non-users (N=142)[a]	Users (N=1,704)[b]
Health problems:		
none	39	44
1	26	31
2	16	11
3	10	8
4 or more	8	7
	100	100
Health status:		
% fair or poor	57	38
Mental health indicators:		
% ever attempted suicide	31	21
% at or above CES-D cutoff of 16	70	49
% with history of mental hospitalization	27	19
Institutionalization		
Incarceration in jail or prison		
none	35	44
one	41	36
both	24	20
	100	100
Mental illness or chemical dependency residential treatment		
none	47	57
one	37	34
both	16	9
	100	100
% with no institutionalizations	28	34

a. No weight possible for nonusers. Percentages based on
unweighted data.
b. Percentages based on weighted data, as the best estimate for
service users.

TABLE 3.16   COMPARISON OF FOOD AND NUTRITION DATA
AMONG HOMELESS PEOPLE WHO DO AND DO
NOT USE SERVICES (percentages)

Food sources	Non-users (N=142)[a]	Users (N=1704)[b]
Mean proportion of time food is obtained from:		
providers	2	76
purchase (grocery, restaurant)	20	12
friends, relatives, handouts	29	6
trash cans	35	1
other	14	5
	100	100
Times person eats per day:		
< 1	15	7
1	51	30
2	27	38
3	6	20
> 3	1	5
	100	100
Number of days in last 7 days without food:		
0	39	64
1	23	19
2	21	9
3	11	5
4 or more	7	3
	100	100
Description of diet		
Get enough of what want to eat	6	19
Get enough, but not what want	25	43
Sometimes do not get enough	30	19
Often do not get enough	40	19
	100	100
Quality of diet		
Rated fair	39	28
Rated poor	39	23

TABLE 3.16   (Continued)

Food sources	Non-users (N=142)[a]	Users (N=1,704)[b]
No consumption of food group during previous day		
Grains	42	30
Meats or meat alternates	37	20
Vegetables/fruits	67	43
Milk and milk products	85	65
Miscellaneous food	43	36
Did not consume any food during previous day	13	8

a. No weight possible for nonusers. Percentages based on unweighted data.
b. Percentages based on weighted data, as the best estimate for service users.

THE HOMELESS OF NEW YORK CITY VERSUS THOSE IN OTHER CITIES

Seventeen percent of our sample of homeless persons were interviewed in New York City. With such a large proportion of the sample coming from a single city that is unique in many ways, it is reasonable to ask in what ways the New York data might influence the results. The answers are very much the same whether one looks at homeless families or at single homeless persons. That is, on important dimensions New York's homeless families and homeless singles are more like each other than like their counterparts elsewhere.

TABLE 3.17   COMPARING NEW YORK TO NON-NEW YORK
RESPONDENTS, ALL RESPONDENTS COMBINED
[weighted percentages (%) and means (M)]

	New York (N=222)	Other cities (N=1482)	All (N=1,704)
With child (%)	22	8	10
Female (%)	34	17	20
< High school (%)	58	46	48
Never married (%)	75	51	55
White (%)	13	52	46
Food stamps:			
now (%)	34	15	18
before (%)	33	43	41
FS per person in household (M)*	$29	$63	$52
% spending no days in shelter	20	25	24
% spending 7 days in shelter	50	31	34
$ from AFDC (%)	9	4	5
$ from GA (%)	30	9	12
$ from working (%)	10	28	25
Self-rating of diet:			
fair (%)	30	28	28
poor (%)	29	22	23
Not enough to eat:			
sometimes (%)	19	19	19
often (%)	19	19	19
Number times eat daily (M)*	1.8	1.9	1.9
NOEATWK[a] = none (%)	73	63	64
TWODAYS[b] = none (%)	71	61	63
Number of servings (M)*	7.6	9.4	9.1
Essential 5 food groups (M)*	2.2	2.8	2.7
Additional food groups (M)*	1.0	1.3	1.3

"N" refers to unweighted data. All figures are based on weighted data.
(M)* indicates means for New York versus other cities differ at p < .05.
a. NOEATWK = number of days without food out of the last seven days.
b. TWODAYS = frequency of going two days without eating.

TABLE 3.17   (Continued)

	New York (N=222)	Other cities (N=1,482)	All (N=1,704)
$ last month (M)*	$253	$147	$162
$ per person last month (M)*	$186	$129	$137
# months homeless (M)*	47.8	36.8	38.5
# days eat at soup kitchen (M)*	2.9	2.4	2.5
# days eat at shelter (M)*	2.2	2.8	2.7
Depression/demoralization (M)*	19.4	16.2	16.7
Mental hospitalization (%)	22	18	19
Drug/alcohol treatment (%)	35	32	33
Time in jail (%)	48	53	52
Time in prison (%)	30	23	24
# types of institution:			
0 (%)	35	34	34
1 (%)	29	27	27
2 (%)	14	22	21
3 (%)	13	14	14
4 (%)	9	3	4

"N" refers to unweighted data. All figures are based on weighted data.
(M)* indicates means for New York versus other cities differ at p < .05.

The homeless in our sample from New York City are more likely than those from the 19 other cities to be non-white, never-married, receiving GA, homeless longer, more depressed/demoralized, and to report more money per person during the past month. They are less likely to have worked during the past month. They report eating fewer servings of all foods and foods from fewer of the five essential food groups during the day before the interview. They are also less likely to eat at either soup kitchens or shelters.

Finally, New York's single homeless are more likely to have served time in prison than the single homeless elsewhere (see table 3.17).

These differences between New York's homeless and those from other large cities pull our results in the direction of the New York responses. This is especially true for families (3.5 percent of families in our study were from New York) and lessso for singles (New Yorkers comprise only 14 percent of all single homeless in the sample). These differences also suggest that policymakers and researchers should be wary of generalizing from New York's homeless to homeless people elsewhere in the country.

SUMMARY AND IMPLICATIONS

The data presented in this chapter have shown that the homeless population consists of a number of important subgroups with quite different characteristics. Although all have extremely low incomes in their homeless condition, some have *human capital* resources that might help them get back on their feet. Slightly more than half have at least a high school education, and 6 percent are college graduates. One in ten has held a steady job within the past three months, and one in four has worked steadily within the past six months. Homeless people with these personal resources may require little assistance to leave homelessness other than an address to receive mail, a phone to make job contacts, a place to cleanup and leave some clothes, and temporary shelter.

At the other extreme are those without a high school education, and the one out of three homeless people who have not held a steady job in more than four years. Multiple physical health problems and a history of mental hospitalization and chemical dependency treatment are associated with longer periods without a steady job. This association suggests that it is probably unrealistic to expect this type of homeless person to maintain a stable domiciled situation on their own without some level of financial support and, equally important, without some supportive services to help them through personal crises.

Most of the homeless are men, virtually none of whom have children with them. However, among the one out of five homeless adults who are women, approximately half are the heads of homeless families, having at least one child with them in their homeless condition. In many ways homeless women with children are a very different group from both single women and homeless men. They are much less likely to have histories of institutionalization, so they do not have those particular strikes against them. However, about half of these women have never been married; many rely on welfare and have little or no attachment to the labor force. Yet even among homeless women with children, experiences vary, so that the half who have not worked at a steady job for more than two years are balanced by the one out of three who have held a steady job within the past year. For the low-skill, low-education, low-work-experience women with children, support for permanently leaving the homeless condition and becoming self-sufficient will probably resemble current welfare reform efforts--basic skills training, work readiness, job training, job search--plus training in parenting and life management skills.

In addition to their implications for reducing homelessness among those already homeless, our data describing homeless individuals also have implications for the need for immediate services--especially for food assistance and medical care, but also for shelter--among the 29 percent of homeless adults who do not use shelters now or use them quite infrequently. Homeless people with the greatest number of health problems and personal problems (as indexed by institutionalizations in mental hospitals, chemical dependency programs, jails and prisons) are least likely to use shelters. This service-use pattern may not be entirely a matter of personal choice, since some shelters will not serve people who are inebriated, are obviously hallucinating, showing other signs of mental illness, or who are potentially or actually violent. They also eat less adequate diets than people without such problems, partly because they do not make as much use of shelters. Although they are among the most physically vulnerable of the homeless, they appear to be the hardest to serve, and are least likely to receive either shelter or food services.

Notes, chapter 3

1. A very broad confidence interval is associated with the adult estimate (± 42 percent, or ± 81,893); for the children it is much smaller (± 647, or 1.9 percent). Readers should refer to volume II, part 2, section B for a detailed description of sampling and weighting issues that contributed to this estimate.

2. Bureau of the Census, *Statistical Abstracts of the United States: 1987*, tables 17 and 745 (estimated data for 1985); *State and Metropolitan Area Data Book, 1986*, table A. (For 1980 MSA data, the census data most parallel to the jurisdictions from which we drew the homeless sample for this study).

3. Bureau of the Census, *Statistical Abstracts of the United States: 1987*, tables 19 and 745 (estimated data for 1985); *State and Metropolitan Area Data Book, 1986*, table A (for 1980 MSA data). The Census Bureau notes that "Hispanic-origin people may be of any race, reflecting the fact that Hispanics may be included as black, white, or "other" in the Census Bureau's statistics on race.

4. U.S. Department of Commerce, Bureau of the Census. *Current Population Reports: Consumer Income*, Series P-60, No. 158. Statistics calculated from information given in table 9.

5. We cannot interpret these data as reflecting the proportions of homeless who are biological parents or the

total number of children who have homeless parents. These questions were not asked.

6. U.S. House of Representatives Committee on Ways and Means, *Background Material and Data on Programs within the Jurisdiction of the Committee on Ways and Means,* 1988 ed. Committee Print 100-29. 100th Congress, 2nd session, March 24, 1988. Table 1, appendix I, p. 711. Tripling $137/person for a 3-person household yields a monthly income 54 percent of the poverty level for a family of three.

7. National Center for Health Statistics. 1987b. *Current Estimates from the National Health Interview Survey: United States 1986.* Washington, D.C.: NCHS, series 10, #164, for 1986 national data from the National Health Interview Survey, adults aged 18-64. National Center for Health Statistics. 1987a. *Health United States: 1986.* Washington, D.C.: U.S. Government Printing Off   table 39 provides low-income population data from th 1985 National Health Interview Survey, covering all persons aged 4-86[+].

8. Eve Moscicki, National Institute of Mental Health, Center for Epidemiological Studies, personal communication, 1987, citing data from a Background Paper for the Secretary's Task Force on Youth Suicide. Data come from Epidemiological Catchment Area (ECA) studies in 5 major cities.

9. The scale used is a short version of the scale used by the Center for Epidemiological Studies, National Institute of Mental Health scale to measure depression, known as the CES-D scale. The scale was first used in this form with homeless people by the New York Psychiatric Institute, and by Rossi et al., 1986.

10. Only adults were interviewed. Each was asked whether he or she was homeless with children and if so, with how many children. Our estimate of the number of children among the homeless stems from these data, with no further information about the children.

Chapter Four

CHARACTERISTICS OF SOUP KITCHENS
AND SHELTERS

Many services exist to serve the homeless. Chief among these are shelters and soup kitchens, set up to respond to the basic emergency needs for food and for protection from the elements. HUD has conducted two studies of shelters in the United States (Department of Housing and Urban Development 1984, 1989) that produced descriptions of shelter characteristics similar to the information obtained from the Institute's study. In addition, the study produced the only existing description of a nationally representative sample of soup kitchen operations, meal quality, resources, and clients. This information is valuable for the formation of public policy to improve the diets of homeless persons.

For the Institute's study, providers of meals and shelter to the homeless were divided into three groups: (1) shelters that serve meals, (2) shelters that do not serve meals, and (3) soup kitchens. This chapter describes these providers and their affiliation, size, services offered, and sources of food used for meal services. The reader should bear in mind that these data are based on a survey of providers in U.S. cities of 100,000 population or over. Twenty-five percent of the U.S. population lives in these cities, which also have the highest rates of homelessness and more than their proportional share of services for the homeless. For example, as of summer 1988, HUD (Department of Housing and Urban Development 1989) estimates that about 64 percent of the shelter bed capacity in U.S. jurisdictions over 25,000 was found in communities with populations of 250,000 or more, which roughly corresponds to the types of cities contained in our study. The Institute's sample of providers is nationally representative and can be generalized to our universe of cities of 100,000 population or more. It cannot be generalized directly, however, to all the providers of food and shelter for the homeless in the country.

TYPES OF PROVIDERS

As of winter 1987, our estimates indicate that there were almost 3,000 providers of meals and/or shelter for the homeless in cities of 100,000 population or over. The vast majority of providers of food or shelter to the homeless (88 percent) do provide some meals. Almost half (47 percent) are shelters that serve at least one meal a day to their residents. Another 41 percent are soup kitchens. Only 12 percent are shelters that do not serve meals. Table 4.1 shows the relative prevalence of different types of providers.

To be classified as a shelter with meals, a facility had to offer both shelter and at least one meal a day to its residents. Three meals per day was most typical. Shelters with meals also varied within type. Thirty-three percent of shelters with meals (16 percent of the provider sample) were classified as missions. A provider was included in this group if it was operated by an organization that had served the homeless for over 10 years, offered one or more meals to its shelter residents, and if less than half of its client households included children. The vast majority of these providers are affiliated with religious organizations. Family shelters offering meals comprised 17 percent of shelters with meals, and 8 percent of the provider sample. Even if run by a traditional organization or in existence for less than 10 years, a shelter was classified as a family shelter if more than half of the households staying there included children.

TABLE 4.1   NUMBER AND PERCENTAGE OF TYPES OF
PROVIDERS OF FOOD AND SHELTER TO THE
HOMELESS (weighted data)

Type of provider	Number in category	Percentage of category	Percentage of provider sample
Soup kitchens			
Church-affiliated	615	53	21
Shelter-affiliated	390	33	14
Other	159	14	6
	1,164	100	41
Shelters without meals			
Welfare hotels	41	12	1
Voucher hotels	12	3	--[a]
Missions	104	30	3
Temporary	191	55	7
	348	100	12
Shelters with meals			
Missions	446	33	16
Family	230	17	8
Temporary	459	34	16
Battered women's programs	57	4	2
Other	164	12	6
	1,356	100	47[b]
Total:	2,869	--	100

a. Less than 1 percent.
b. Numbers do not add to total due to rounding.

The majority of these were also affiliated with religious organizations.

The largest category of shelters with meals was temporary shelters (34 percent of shelters with meals and 16 percent of all providers in the sample). This category included shelters in existence for less than 10 years, in which less than 50 percent of the adults were accompanied by children, and which were run by any of a variety of organizations--community groups, churches, local governments, labor unions, coalitions for the homeless, housing authorities and similar agencies. Other shelters with meals (12 percent of shelters with meals and 6 percent of the total) were a varied group and included several alcohol rehabilitation programs attached to traditional shelters and, in one city, board and care facilities serving the homeless through local government purchase-of-service agreements. These shelters comprised 12 percent of shelters with meals and 6 percent of the total.

Soup kitchens are the second most prevalent of service providers to the homeless, accounting for 41 percent of all providers in the sample. Over half of these were classified as church-affiliated (21 percent of all providers). Church-affiliated soup kitchens might be affiliated with a church, coalition of churches, denominational social services agencies (such as Catholic Charities or Lutheran Social Services), or with a Catholic or Episcopal diocese.

Most of the rest (33 percent of soup kitchens and 14 percent of all providers) were shelter-affiliated soup kitchens. These are predominantly affiliated with religious organizations as well. They differ from providers classified as church-affiliated soup kitchens in being operated by a shelter which typically served one meal at which most users were *not* shelter residents.

Shelters without meals are the smallest group (12 percent of all service providers to the homeless). A shelter without meals was considered a mission if it was operated by an organization that had served the homeless for more than 10 years. These shelters were also affiliated with traditional national organizations such as the Salvation Army, St.

Vincent De Paul Society, or mission associations; the category included YWCAs and YMCAs if they provided rooms for the homeless and did not serve meals. This type of shelter comprised 30 percent of shelters without meals, and 3 percent of all providers in the sample.

A shelter without meals was classified as temporary if it had existed for only a few years and did not fall into the other categories of shelters without meals. These types of shelters comprised 55 percent of shelters without meals, and 7 percent of the provider sample. They were run by a variety of organizations including local governments, settlement houses, churches, and community groups. Welfare hotels and voucher hotels are both very small groups, constituting only 12 percent and 3 percent of shelters without meals, respectively, and under 2 percent of all providers of services to the homeless.

GROWTH OF SOUP KITCHEN AND SHELTER FACILITIES IN THE 1980s

Shelters for the homeless prior to the 1980s were typically missions, serving a largely single male alcoholic population. Services for the homeless have expanded greatly in both number and type since the 1980s began. In March 1987 an estimated 1,160 soup kitchens and 1,700 shelters served the homeless in U.S. cities with 100,000 population or more (table 4.1).

More than half of the providers in every category were less than 9 years old and did not exist prior to 1981 (see table 4.2). Thirty-eight percent of soup kitchens, 41 percent of shelters that serve meals, and 32 percent of shelters that do not serve meals were 4 years old or less in 1987. At the other extreme, 14 percent of soup kitchens, 18 percent of shelters with meals and 7 percent of shelters without meals had been in operation for 21 or more years in 1987.

Not only have the numbers of facilities expanded greatly during the decade, but overall capacity has expanded as

TABLE 4.2   YEARS IN SERVICE AMONG DIFFERENT TYPES
OF PROVIDERS (weighted percentages)

	Type of provider			
Years in service as of 1987	Soup kitchens (N=151)	Shelters with meals (N=46)	Shelters without meals (N=184)	Totals (N=381)
< 2 years	26	19	11	21
2-4 years	12	22	21	18
5-8 years	26	18	45	24
9-20 years	23	23	16	22
21+ years	14	18	7	15
Totals	100	100	100	100
Mean	13	16	10	18
Median	6	6	5	6
Range	0 - 114	0 - 114	0 - 87	0 - 114

"N" refers to unweighted data. All percentages are based on
weighted data.

well. HUD estimated in 1983 that 98,000 adults and
children could be housed per night in emergency shelters
(this figure excludes facilities for runaway and homeless
youth; Department of Housing and Urban Development
1984, p. 34). Figures from HUD's 1988 survey indicate that
capacity has grown to 275,000 beds in emergency shelters
(Department of Housing and Urban Development 1989, p. 2).

From the data on shelter and meal operations supplied
by providers in the Institute's study, we were able to
estimate the number of shelter beds and the number of
prepared meals available to the homeless in cities of over
100,000 population (see table 4.3). There were almost
120,000 shelter beds available in U.S. cities of 100,000
population or more in March 1987; 70 percent of these beds

TABLE 4.3   ESTIMATED NUMBER OF BEDS PER NIGHT AND
NUMBER OF MEALS PER DAY AVAILABLE FROM
SERVICE PROVIDERS, IN CITIES OF 100,000
POPULATION OR MORE, BY PROVIDER TYPE
(weighted data)

| Service provided | Type of provider | | Totals (N=230) |
	Shelters without meals (N=46)	Shelters with meals (N=184)	
Total number of beds provided			
Number	35,610	84,026	119,637
Percentage	30	70	100
95% confidence interval	± 5431	± 5858	± 8,062
Range			
Low	30,179	78,168	111,575
High	41,041	89,884	127,699

| Total number of meals served | Type of provider | | Totals (N=335) |
	Soup kitchens (N=151)	Shelters with meals (N=184)	
Number	97,112	224,039	321,152
Percentage	30	70	100
95% confidence interval	± 5,904	± 13,850	± 15,561
Range			
Low	103,016	237,889	336,713
High	91,208	210,189	305,591

"N" refers to unweighted data. All figures are based on weighted data. The estimate of soup kitchen meals given in this table equals 57 percent of all meals served at soup kitchens, to adjust for the fact that in our data collection with homeless individuals, only 57 percent of those contacted at soup kitchens were homeless. Estimates for both soup kitchens and shelters have been adjusted to account for providers who operate fewer than seven days a week.

were located in shelters that serve meals. Juxtaposing HUD's 1988 and the Institute's 1988 figures (275,000 versus 120,000) suggests that almost half of this country's emergency shelter capacity is located in its 178 largest cities, although only about 25 percent of the U.S. population resides in these cities.

There is no estimate from the early 1980s of the number of meals available to the homeless, so comparisons over time cannot be made. However, from data collected in the Institute's study we estimate that in large U.S. cities in March 1987, soup kitchens and shelters served the homeless about 321,000 meals per day. Seventy percent were served by shelters and the remaining 30 percent by soup kitchens (see table 4.3). (The same soup kitchens served an additional 73,000 meals per day to persons who were hungry but not homeless.)

Despite the expansion in emergency services for the homeless during the 1980s, however, the existing services do not meet the need. Our estimate indicates that there were 194,000 homeless adults and 35,000 homeless children who used either soup kitchens or shelters in large U.S. cities in March 1987. The 120,000 available shelter beds supply slightly less than half of the beds needed for this total of 229,000 homeless persons who use services; the 321,000 meals a day provided an average of 1.4 meals per person, per day among service users. The average number of meals consumed per day by homeless adults in this study was 1.9, meaning that the soup kitchen and shelter meals supplied most of the daily food intake of these service-using homeless people, but could not provide the homeless with the 3-meals-plus per day that is the daily intake of the average American.

The gap in shelter and food services is even wider than these figures indicate, because an additional unknown number of homeless people exist in the cities surveyed who do not use soup kitchens or shelters at all. Their needs are as great or greater than those of service users (see tables 3.14, 3.15 and 3.16). Further, available research indicates that most homeless people in rural areas do not use services because none are available (Roth et al. 1985).

TABLE 4.4 SERVICES OTHER THAN FOOD AND SHELTER
OFFERED BY PROVIDERS OF DIFFERENT TYPES
(weighted percentages)

	Type of provider			
Type of service	Soup kitchens (N=151)	Shelters with meals (N=46)	Shelters without meals (N=184	Totals (N=381)
Clothing	56	93	54	73
Health care referrals	45	91	88	72
Shower/bath/shave	19	93	83	62
Mail receiving	24	90	84	62
Social work/counseling	30	80	85	60
Carfare/transportation	29	69	80	54
Legal services	21	71	52	48
Job training/placement	26	63	51	47
Personal storage	9	71	61	45
Religious services	45	56	2	45
Laundry	14	68	48	44
Recreation	16	63	50	42
Job placement	19	48	39	35
Health care on-site	17	28	44	25
Child care/ community outreach	14	28	19	21
Education/GED/workshops	5	21	8	13
Housing referrals	6	15	24	12
Access to free telephone	8	10	10	9
Financial assistance	3	10	12	7

"N" refers to unweighted data. All percentages are based on weighted data.

TABLE 4.5   DISTRIBUTION OF PROVIDERS OF DIFFERENT
TYPES AND SIZES (weighted percentages)

Size of provider	Type of provider			
	Soup kitchens (N=151)	Shelters without meals (N=46)	Shelters with meals (N=184)	Totals (N=381)
Serving 10-25	28	36	25	27
Serving 26-50	17	15	30	23
Serving 51-99	21	31	30	27
Serving 100+	34	17	15	23
	100	99	100	100

"N" refers to unweighted data. All percentages are based on
weighted data. Percentages may not sum to 100 due to rounding.

SERVICES OFFERED BY PROVIDERS

In addition to meals and shelter, the typical provider offered
homeless clients a number of other services. Table 4.4
shows the variety of these services and the frequency with
which providers make them available. The additional
services most commonly offered are clothing and health care
referrals, followed by bathing facilities, mail receiving, and
social work/counseling. Nine out of ten shelters offer six or
more services in addition to shelter and meals. Soup
kitchens are much less likely to have a wide range of services
available; 62 percent offer only one to five services in
addition to meals.

Soup kitchens serve the largest number of clients on
average, with just over one-third serving 100 or more clients

TABLE 4.6   NUMBER OF DAYS PER WEEK MEALS ARE
SERVED AND NUMBER OF MEALS SERVED
PER DAY, BY PROVIDER TYPE (weighted
percentages)

Frequency of meal provision	Type of provider		Totals (N=335)
	Soup kitchens (N=151)	Shelters with meals (N=184)	
Number of days per week that provider serves meals			
One	15	0	7
Two	7	0	3
Three	7	2	4
Four	5	1	3
Five	19	2	9
Six	14	3	8
Seven	32	92	65
	100	100	100
Number of meals per day that provider serves			
One	72	11	38
Two	25	35	30
Three	3	54	31
	100	100	100

"N" refers to unweighted data of providers in the sample. All
percentages are based on weighted data.

per meal and 72 percent serving at least 26 clients per meal. Shelters with meals were typically in the middle-size range, with only 15 percent serving 100 or more persons per day, but 75 percent serving at least 26 (see table 4.5).

Meal Services Offered, Meal Variety and Nutrient Content

The number of meals served per day differs substantially between shelters that serve meals and soup kitchens (see table 4.6). Over half the shelters that serve meals (54 percent) serve three meals a day; in contrast, only 3 percent of soup kitchens do so. Almost three-quarters of soup kitchens (72 percent) serve only one meal a day, compared with only 11 percent of shelters that serve meals. Shelters that serve meals are also much more likely to do so seven days a week than are soup kitchens. More than 9 out of 10 shelters with meals serve every day, whereas one out of two soup kitchens serve five days a week or less. Because of these differences in frequency, more than twice as many meals per day are served to the homeless in shelters as in soup kitchens (see table 4.3).

The same persons who interviewed providers in the Institute's study also observed meal variety. Observations involved recording foods served and making judgments about the size of portions and the contents of casseroles and other mixed dishes. These detailed observations permit analysis of the food *served*, by food group and by nutrient and caloric availability.[1] Time and budget limitations did not permit data collection on the types or amounts of food actually *eaten* or plate waste. Therefore the following description of the meals served may not be the same in quantity and variety as the food the homeless actually consumed. In addition, proportionally fewer breakfasts and proportionally more lunches and dinners were observed than providers actually served, so observations were not representative of provider meals in a strict statistical sense. This sampling pattern results in an upward bias in estimates of food group and nutrient content of the average provider meal, since the average breakfast is somewhat lower on the number of essential food groups represented, calories, and protein than lunch or dinner. On the other hand, the average provider breakfast does contain more of certain nutrients than the other two meals; therefore any bias is likely to be small.[2]

Presence of Certain Food Groups

The analysis was based on 10 food groups, five of which are considered essential for an adequate diet and should be eaten daily (Human Nutrition Information Service 1986). Certain additional foods such as baked goods and sweets provide few vitamins and minerals, but they do provide needed calories. Fats and oils provide essential fatty acids and certain other nutrients in addition to calories.

Essential	Additional
Milk and milk products	Fats and oils
Grain products	Baked goods
Fruits and fruit juices	Sweets
Vegetables	Sweetened beverages
Meat and meat alternates	Salty snacks

The meals typically available to the homeless, particularly lunch and dinner, provide substantial variety. A majority of lunches and dinners (55 and 51 percent, respectively) contained at least four of the five essential food groups, and 8 out of 10 lunches and dinners contained at least one of the additional five food groups. Breakfast was the only meal at which any providers served less than two essential food groups, and this only applied to 10 percent of the breakfasts. It should also be noted that 28 percent of providers included at least four essential food groups even at breakfast. The mean number of essential food groups served at breakfast was 2.9, at lunch 3.6, and at dinner 3.6. All meal types also included an average of 1.3 food groups from the additional groups.

Nutrient Content

The meals provided to the homeless were assessed for 13 nutrients:

Protein (grams)   Vitamin B-6 (mg)
Carbohydrates (grams)   Vitamin A (IU)
Fat (grams)   Iron (mg)
Vitamin C (mg)   Magnesium (mg)
Thiamin (mg)   Calcium (mg)
Riboflavin (mg)   Phosphorus (mg)
Niacin (mg)

All but two of these (carbohydrates and fat) have recommended dietary allowances (RDAs) for both men and women, to which the content of meals available to the homeless was compared.[3]

On this measure, too, the average availability of nutrients in provider meals is quite high (see table 4.7). The average meal provided over 50 percent of the RDA for both men and women for 7 of the 11 nutrients: protein, vitamin C, thiamin, riboflavin, niacin, vitamin A, and phosphorous. Of these nutrients, protein, thiamin, phosphorus, vitamin A, and vitamin C were available in the average meal in amounts between 70 and 100 percent of the RDA for both men and women; riboflavin and niacin were available in amounts between 51 and 75 percent of the RDA for both men and women. The only nutrients for which 50 percent or less of the RDA for men and women was provided were calcium, Vitamin B-6, and magnesium. Iron was available at 70 percent of the RDA for men, but only 39 percent of the RDA for women. It should be noted that the average American has a relatively low dietary intake of vitamin C, calcium, and iron. Meals for the homeless appear to be quite high in vitamin C, however. The reader should note that RDAs are for individuals 19-50 years of age, and refer to recommendations for *a whole day's* consumption, whereas

TABLE 4.7 AVERAGE NUTRIENT CONTENT OF BREAKFASTS, LUNCHES, AND DINNERS OFFERED BY SOUP KITCHENS AND SHELTERS, BY NUTRIENT

Nutrient	Type of meal				RDAs[a]	
	Breakfast (N=45)	Lunch (N=135)	Dinner (N=128)	Average meal (N=308)	Men	Women
Protein (grams)	31	37	48	41	56	44
Carbohydrates (grams)	93	113	138	122	n.a.	n.a.
Fat (grams)	34	39	47	42	n.a.	n.a.
Vitamin C (mg)	43	39	54	46	60	60
Thiamin (mg)	1	1	1	1	1.4	1
Riboflavin (mg)	1	1	1	1	1.6	1.2
Niacin (mg)	12	9	12	10	18	13
Vitamin B-6 (mg)	1	1	1	1	2.2	2
Vitamin A (IU)	2,279	3,601	5,840	4,557	5,000	4,000
Iron (mg)	9	7	8	7	10	18
Magnesium (mg)	119	98	118	110	350	300
Calcium (mg)	359	353	445	403	800	800
Phosphorus (mg)	571	525	624	579	800	800
Calories	803	973	1,153	1,023	2,700	2,000

"N" refers to unweighted data of meals observed. All figures are based on weighted data.
a. RDAs are for individuals 19-50 years of age, and refer to recommendations for a *whole day's* consumption. Figures for provider meals refer to the nutrients available in *one average meal*.

the data for provider meals refer to the nutrients available in *one average meal.*

Providers mentioned that they deliberately tried to enrich their meals with as much food of high nutritional value as possible given their resources, knowing that the people eating their meals may not get another meal that day. As discussed earlier, interviews with homeless individuals indicate that they eat 1.9 meals a day, on average, with those who only use soup kitchens eating significantly fewer meals than those who use shelters (1.6 versus 2.0 meals). So providers are right to enrich their meals as much as possible; the eating patterns reported by homeless service users suggest that they need meals high in nutrient value.

Caloric Content

As would be expected, the caloric content of the meal differed by type of meal, with breakfast averaging the least (803 calories) and dinner the most (1,153 calories). When breakfasts, lunches, and dinners are combined, the estimated mean number of calories per meal averages 1,023, with a median of 920. Twenty-five percent of meals had caloric values of 690 or less, and 25 percent had caloric values of 1,218 and above. The average meal of 1,023 calories provides 38 percent of the recommended daily level of 2,700 for adult men and 51 percent of the recommended daily level of 2,000 for adult women (see table 4.7).

The number of calories offered in the average meal tended to be lower for the larger providers. Twice as many large providers (serving over 100 people per day) as small providers (serving less than 26 people per day), for example, served meals of under 500 calories, despite the fact that the meals we observed at these providers were more likely to be lunches or dinners. And small providers were much more likely to serve meals in the highest calorie category (1,525 calories or more) than were large providers. In the intermediate calorie categories, size of provider made less difference. Several explanations may exist; one possibility is that large providers are stretching limited resources to serve more people.

SOURCES OF SUPPORT FOR HOMELESS SERVICES

Throughout the decade of the 1980s, as homelessness has increased around the country, the federal government maintained the position that homelessness was a local problem and that solutions would have to be found at the local level. It is not surprising therefore that for most of the decade a very great proportion of the support, both financial and in-kind, for services for the homeless has come from sources other than government. Government has been increasing its contributions in the last few years, mainly in the area of financial support for shelters. But individuals, religious congregations, charitable organizations, United Way, businesses, and foundations still provide most of the labor and other goods and services (for example, donated food, donated space) that allow services for the homeless to function.

In 1987 Congress acted to involve federal resources for the first time in programs directed exclusively toward the homeless, for the first time, passing the McKinney Act with a heavy concentration on funding for shelter facilities. Specific breakdowns of sources of support are only available nationwide from three sources: HUD's 1983 and 1988 surveys (for shelter costs) and the Institute's study (for food service costs).

Support for Shelters

HUD reported that 63 percent of shelter operating expenses in 1983 ($138 million) were paid for with private resources, while 37 percent came from government ($56 million). In addition, volunteers supplemented paid staff such that in 1983, four volunteers served in homeless shelters for every three paid staff persons. HUD calculated the value of these volunteer hours at $31 million, using the minimum wage as the value of an hour of donated labor (Department of Housing and Urban Development, 1984, pp. 42-3). The value of many other donations was not calculated, including free space, donated food, clothing and supplies, and free professional services.

A 1988 repeat of HUD's research indicates that significant shifts have taken place in sources of support for shelter services. Thirty-five percent of shelter operating expenses in 1988 came from private sources, while 65 percent came from government--a reversal of the 1983 pattern. The dollar value of these expenses had risen from $138 million of private support to $560 million, and from $56 million of government support to $1.04 billion. This represents a fourfold increase for private support and an 18- to 19-fold increase in government support. About one-fourth of the total government support probably came from the federal government through McKinney Act programs ($180 million for shelter programs in FFY 1987, which was spent mostly in 1988, and $73 million in FFY 1988), implying that three-fourths of the total government financial support for shelter operations comes from the state and local government levels.

The ratio of volunteers to paid staff in shelters shifted to approximately two volunteers for each full- or part-time paid staff person, and the estimated value of volunteer time rose to $100 million by 1988--a threefold increase (Department of Housing and Urban Development, 1989, pp. 17-20).

Support for Meal Services

The Urban Institute's study looked at the sources of support for meal services, whether provided at soup kitchens or in shelters. (The resources attributable to shelter-based meal services overlap to an unknown degree with the supports for shelters in HUD's 1988 study, since many of the shelters in HUD's study also served meals and HUD's assessment of their resources included resources used to provide meals.)

Thirty-five percent of meal services in soup kitchens and shelters operate with *no* paid staff. Twenty-three percent used 1-20 volunteer hours per week, 18 percent used 21-40 volunteer hours per week, 10 percent used between one and two full-time equivalents, and 33 percent operated with more than two full-time equivalents of volunteer time (14 percent had more than five volunteer full-time equivalents). Volunteers supplied 58 percent of the hours devoted to food preparation, service, and cleanup in soup kitchens and shelters. Volunteer hours represented a value of donated labor of approximately $5 million a year, calculated using the minimum wage.

Paid staff time devoted to meal service had a value estimated by providers to be about the same amount, $5 million, during the most recent program year (usually, 1986). Eighteen percent of the providers had paid staff working between 1 and 20 hours per week, 14 percent had between a half-time and a full-time equivalent of paid staff, and none had more than five full-time equivalents of paid staff.

The substantial use of volunteers does not mean that the providers are staffed with persons who have no food service experience, however. Three-quarters of the providers serving meals indicated that at least one person among their paid staff, volunteers, or board of directors had food service experience or training; more than one-quarter reported more than one person with such training. The most common type of experience was as a cook in a restaurant or as a restaurant owner (63 percent of all meal providers); 17 percent had staff with some training in nutrition or dietetics.

Sources of Food for Meal Services

Table 4.8 indicates that purchased food was a major source for about half of these meal providers. Fifty-six percent said that purchased food (either retail or wholesale) was their first or second largest source, and 82 percent purchased some food. About one out of four providers relied on purchased food for more than half of the food they served. However, 18 percent of providers did not purchase any food for their meal

TABLE 4.8   RELIANCE OF MEAL PROVIDERS ON DIFFERENT
SOURCES OF FOOD (weighted percentages;
N = 335)[a]

Degree of reliance on food source	Percentage using food source			
	Purchase	USDA commod-ities	Food banks[b]	Private donations
Get *any* food from this source	82	67	69	88
This source is the first or second largest source of food	56	35	34	39
Get more than half of their food from this source	26	3	10	21

a. "N" refers to unweighted data. All percentages in this table are
based on weighted data.
b. "Food Banks" is *exclusive* of USDA commodities, although such
commodities may also be distributed by Food Banks.

services--all food used came from commodities provided by
the USDA food banks, and donations from individuals,
businesses, churches, United Way, and other organizations.

The relative importance of different food sources is
shown in table 4.8. Most shelters serving meals and soup
kitchens appear to be tied into federal commodity
distribution programs; 67 percent got some food from this
source.[4] But only 35 percent of meal providers listed USDA
commodities as one of their two largest sources of food, and
only three percent relied on commodities for more than half
of the food they served. The picture for food banks is
similar, with food banks providing the first or second largest
source of food for 34 percent of meal providers, while 69
percent reported getting at least some food from food banks.

Almost all meal providers (88 percent) got some food from donations, but only 39 percent listed donations as their first or second largest source of food. One in five meal providers relied on donations to supply more than half of the food they served; among those who listed donations as their first or second largest source, slightly more than half got more than 50 percent of their food from donations.

Where meal providers get food has some bearing on the variety and nutrient content of the food they serve (based on analysis of systematic observations of 308 provider meals). The higher the proportion of food that comes from USDA commodities, the more calories, protein, carbohydrates, vitamin C, vitamin B-6, thiamin, riboflavin, niacin, iron, magnesium, calcium, and phosphorus their meals contained. USDA commodities also contributed more servings of milk products, vegetables, and grains, and more food groups from the five essential food groups. Higher proportions of purchased food were associated with less protein and fat, and fewer servings of milk products. The heavier the reliance on donations, the fewer servings of vegetables and grain products were present in meals, and the lower meals were in carbohydrates, thaimin, niacin, vitamin B-6, iron and magnesium. Meat and meat alternates appear to be the only foods that increase when the proportion of donated foods increases. Altogether, it appears that the homeless benefit most in terms of nutrition when the providers they frequent make more extensive use of USDA commodity programs.

Sources of Cash Income for Meal Services

Cash donations from individuals in the community were the most substantial source of cash; four out of five providers received some cash from individuals, with 59 percent citing them as their first or second largest source and 38 percent getting more than half of their cash from individual donors (see table 4.9).

Churches and government were next. Although 68 percent of meal providers got some cash from church contributions, compared to only 45 percent from government sources, approximately equal numbers cited churches and government as their first or second largest source. One-third of those that got any government money got more than half of their cash from government. Twenty-nine percent of providers mentioned federal government sources of cash for meal services, but only 6 percent listed federal funds as their first or second source of cash; the Emergency Food and Shelter Program, administered by FEMA, was the primary federal source.

Nongovernment organizations, such as United Way, corporations, and charitable foundations, were a source of cash for meal services for about half of these meal providers. However, fewer than one in four cited this source as one of their two largest, and very few (5 percent) got more than half of their cash from these non-government organizations. Charges to users of meal services turned out to be a very small item; 84 percent did not have user charges at all, and only 3 percent relied on them for more than half of their cash income.

The two biggest sources of food account, on average, for 88 percent of all food used (median = 94 percent). The two biggest sources of cash account for 86 percent of all cash received for meal services (median = 90 percent). Therefore, the remaining sources of food or cash, although potentially numerous, contribute only 12-14 percent, on average, of the food or cash used by providers of meals for the homeless. Further, for only 1 percent of all providers did the two largest sources of cash account for less than 50 percent of all cash received, and for less than half of 1 percent of all providers did the two largest sources of food account for less than 50 percent of all food received.

Cost Per Meal

The average provider's cost for food served per meal varied between $0.36 and $0.58. Soup kitchens' average cost for food per meal was lower than for shelters ($0.39 versus

TABLE 4.9   RELIANCE OF MEAL PROVIDERS ON DIFFERENT SOURCES OF CASH INCOME FOR MEAL SERVICES (weighted percentages; N = 335)[a]

| Degree of reliance on cash source | Percentage using source of cash income | | | | |
	Charges to users	Churches	Individuals	Nongovernment organizations[b]	Government
Get *any* cash from this source	16	68	80	53	45
This source is the first or second largest source of cash	5	33	59	23	30
Get more than half of their cash from this source	3	9	38	5	15

a. "N" refers to unweighted data. All percentages are based on weighted data.

b. Such as United Way, corporations, foundations.

$0.56). Larger providers paid less per meal, on average, than smaller providers. It must be remembered that many of these providers relied on substantial amounts of donated food which, on average, augmented the *value* of the food served to approximately three times the actual cash outlays for food. Provider food budgets varied from a low of nothing (5 percent of all providers) to over $1 million (in a large, city-run shelter where meals were supplied through a catering contract). Twelve percent of all meal providers had food budgets in excess of $40,000 in 1986. However, fully one in four providers serving more than 100 people per meal, per day had food expenses of less than $5,000 for the whole year of 1986. These figures testify to how much can be done with extremely limited funds.

SUMMARY AND IMPLICATIONS

The 1980s saw a tremendous growth in services for the homeless. Half of all shelters and soup kitchens operating in early 1987 did not exist at the beginning of the decade, and shelter bed capacity almost tripled between 1983 and 1988. The involvement of the private, voluntary sector in providing these services is enormous; until the past few years most of the cash for shelter and meal services came from private sources, as did a very large proportion of the labor through the commitment of volunteers. Much of this private activity seems also to be religiously motivated; more than three out of four shelters or soup kitchens are affiliated with a religious congregation or organization. Some of these providers operate as traditional missionary organizations interested, as the Salvation Army's slogan puts it, in "soup, soap, and salvation." Other congregations and individuals are responding out of the charity prescribed by their religious tenets, to help people in need. The plight of the homeless has clearly called forth intense activity and involvement in the religious community, which has played a very significant role in expanding services for the homeless.

It is also clear that the public sector became a bigger player in financing services for the homeless towards the end of the 1980s. As services have expanded, so have the resources necessary to run them. Government at all levels is providing an increasingly larger share of these additional resources. The 1983 pattern of private interests supplying two-thirds of the money to run shelters has reversed itself; in 1988 governments supplied two-thirds of this cash. At the same time, the expansion of private financial and other commitments has continued. The inability of the private sector to meet the need and its intense lobbying of local, state, and federal governments to meet public welfare obligations has undoubtedly been responsible for much of the expansion in government involvement in the late 1980s.

Notes, chapter 4

1. For a description of the methods used to collect and analyze meal observation data and individual intake data, see part 2, section E of *Supplementary Statistics and Methodological Documentation* (Burt and Cohen 1988b, volume II).

2. The distribution of meals at which interviewers did observations was 15 percent breakfasts, 44 percent midday meals, and 41 percent evening meals. This compares to a distribution of all meals served that is approximately 29 percent breakfasts, 32 percent midday meals and 39 percent evening meals.

3. The recommended dietary allowances (RDAs) and recommended energy intake (REI, or calories) are established by the Food and Nutrition Board of the National Academy of Sciences (National Research Council 1980). These are not minimum requirements but rather average daily amounts of nutrients and energy (calories) that meet the known nutritional needs of nearly all healthy people. Because the

needs of individuals vary, intakes below the RDA or REI are not necessarily inadequate. Although the relationship may not be straightforward, the risk of some individuals having inadequate intakes may increase, the further intakes fall below the RDA or REI (U.S. Department of Human Services and U.S. Department of Agriculture, 1986).

4. The U.S. Department of Agriculture distributes surplus farm products to eligible recipients through several different mechanisms. Commodities have traditionally been dairy products (cheese, butter) and grain products (such as flour, cornmeal, and oatmeal). The commodities distribution programs have always had a dual purpose--to dispose of surplus farm products and to serve needy recipients. The former purpose has had the most influence, but there are some circumstances in which the USDA purchases additional commodities such as canned meats and fruits to augment the limited fare available through surplus. The school breakfast and lunch programs have received these additional commodities for some time. The Hunger Prevention Act of 1988 appropriated money for the first time to permit USDA to purchase and distribute these additional commodities to meal programs that serve the homeless.

Chapter Five

STATE AND FEDERAL ACTIVITIES

Earlier chapters have described urban homeless adults who use services, and the nature of the services they use. Many of these services have been developed by private organizations and individuals, in response to local perceptions of need, relying heavily on private resources. But homelessness is more than a local problem, and some solutions lie beyond the capacities of local or private resources, which so far have focused almost exclusively on meeting emergency needs for food and shelter. Little energy or resources have remained for long-term approaches or prevention efforts, even though many providers and advocates understand that their activities represent first aid rather than cure.

Government action is increasingly needed both short term to fund emergency and transitional services for homeless people, and long term, to *prevent* homelessness. Government also has other potential: to serve a planning and coordinating function, to develop a sophisticated understanding of what is needed to eliminate homelessness, to create needed resources through its legislative powers, and to allocate these resources where they are needed.

This chapter presents information gathered during the summer of 1988 in six states: California, Connecticut, Georgia, New Mexico, Ohio, and Wisconsin (Burt and Cohen 1988c). The Urban Institute conducted field visits under a contract with the federal Interagency Council on the Homeless, with the purpose of describing state programs and activities for the homeless and the supports and barriers to

further program development. The states have extremely
varied levels of commitment to homeless issues and quite
different approaches to the problem. Many state activities
are quite innovative, and all may be interesting to
policymakers looking for what has been tried and what
works.

STATE POLICY DEVELOPMENT AND COORDINATION

We first examine how states have organized themselves to
address the issue of homelessness and to increase their level
of planning and coordination to meet the needs of the
homeless population. We then look at the nongovernment,
state-level organizations concerned with issues surrounding
the homeless. This information illustrates a variety of
workable approaches to coordination.

Three of the states we visited, California, Connecticut,
and Ohio, had state-level coordinating councils, task forces,
or working groups prior to the passage of the McKinney Act.
These organizations involved state agency staff in issues of
homelessness and programs to solve them. In these three
states, active, statewide nongovernment organizations or
coalitions focused on homeless issues had also existed prior
to the McKinney Act. The remaining three states, Georgia,
New Mexico, and Wisconsin, were not organized at the state
level prior to the act (Georgia still does not have a state
agency task force or coordinating group) and do not, even
now, have statewide nongovernment coalitions for the
homeless.

The six states visited have developed several different
types of coordinating bodies to deal with issues of
homelessness. These task forces, councils, and working
groups share information and often work on coordinated
planning and program implementation. However, none of
the coordinating bodies has any power over its
members--neither the group as a whole nor the lead agency
can *require* a member agency to act in a certain way.

Information-sharing, discussion, persuasion, bargaining, follow-up reminders of promises made, and sometimes offers of assistance to complete tasks are the modes of influence used. The primary types of coordinating bodies described here are:

+ a task force or working group comprised exclusively of state agency representatives;

+ a task force, council or work group that includes representatives from state agencies and also from local governments, the federal government, and/or private providers, advocates, or their statewide organizations; and,

+ a statewide coalition of advocates and providers of services to the homeless (such as Coalition for the Homeless, Coalition Against Domestic Violence).

Coordinating Bodies Limited to State Agencies

Three states have task forces or working groups comprised exclusively of state agency representatives: the California Task Force, the Connecticut State Work Group, and the New Mexico McKinney Task Force. Each of the three was formed after passage of the McKinney Act in July 1987, for the purpose of taking lead responsibility in coordinating state efforts with respect to McKinney Act funding. Two states, California and Connecticut, also have task forces with broader representation that pre-date these more restricted working groups.

It is instructive to look at these coordinating bodies, which state agency assumes the lead role, and which state agencies are active. In each state the lead agency is the health and welfare/human services/human resources department. Departments of mental health, social services, employment/labor, and education are represented in all three states. Departments of aging, alcohol and drug programs, housing, veterans affairs, and corrections/criminal justice are present in two of the three states. Departments of health, food/agriculture, children and youth, and income maintenance are each present in only one state.

Note that the lead agency for each of these coordinating bodies is a health and welfare/human services/human resources department--*not* a housing department. In one state (New Mexico), the housing department is not even a member of the task force. The agency taking the lead generally administers a variety of programs needed by the homeless; and agency personnel commonly have a good idea of the complexity of the problems of homeless people and what it will take to reduce homelessness. They are also the agencies *interested* in taking the lead--the agencies that want to see statewide coordination and program expansion to address the issues surrounding the homeless. This pattern--the low profile assumed by housing agencies contrasted with the key role played by human services agencies--is reflected as well in the other task force structures described in the next section.

Coordinating Bodies with State Agencies and Other Members

Four of the states we visited had coordinating bodies that included representatives from local governments, from the private sector, and from federal agencies. They included California's Working Group on the Homeless, established in July 1985; Connecticut's Governor's Task Force on the Homeless, which functioned from 1983 to 1986; Ohio's Homeless Cluster that began in 1985; and, Wisconsin's Homeless Work Group, the newest of the set, established in 1987.

The California Working Group on the Homeless. The California Working Group on the Homeless was established in July

1985. It initially had no staff and met every other month, primarily to share information. Its first convener was the HUD regional coordinator; its current convener is the director of the California/Nevada Community Action Association, known as CAL-NEVA. When CAL-NEVA took over, the state was not interested in taking on the role of convener, but did provide some in-kind assistance to the working group.

The working group is composed of representatives from state government agencies, representatives from local government organizations, federal government regional representatives, and representatives from statewide private nonprofit agencies. It was named in the state Comprehensive Homeless Assistance Plan (or CHAP--required by the McKinney Act) as the coordinating council for the state, and the state has used it to identify problems and resources. It has also served as the vehicle through which information and funding opportunities can be disseminated quickly to relevant agencies throughout the state.

Connecticut's Governor's Task Force on the Homeless.
Connecticut established its Governor's Task Force on the Homeless in 1983. In that year a radio disk jockey, who was also a member of a shelter board in Hartford, spoke to the governor and convinced him of the importance of the issue of homelessness. In October 1983 the governor formed the task force, with the Department of Human Resources providing staff support. The Connecticut Governor's Task Force representatives came from state and local government agencies and the private sector. About half of the membership came from the private sector. The Task Force held public hearings and commissioned a survey of town officials, which showed a marked discrepancy in ideas about the scope of the problem. Approximately one-third of town officials surveyed did not think that homelessness existed. That perception has changed over the years.

In February 1985 the Governor's Task Force on the Homeless issued a final report. The conclusions were that government, in conjunction with the private sector, should respond to the immediate need for temporary shelter and also develop programs to address the root causes of homelessness. The governor designated the Department of Human Resources as the lead agency for emergency shelter programs and services to the homeless. He designated the Department of Housing as the lead agency for housing issues for the homeless. The task force continued its work and developed the Governor's Task Force Action Plan, published in January 1986, which spelled out specific tasks for specific groups. The office of Policy and Management followed up to see if designated groups were accomplishing their goals.

Ohio's Homeless Cluster. Ohio's state government structure is very complex, with a variety of departments and divisions. Ohio's governor has used the concept of interdepartmental groupings and "clusters" to organize the various departments for action on specific issues. The Homeless Cluster primarily shares information and alerts providers to funding possibilities. While the cluster oversees the state-administered McKinney Act monies, the Ohio Coalition for the Homeless, an association of advocates and providers, has done most of the tracking of the flow of funds. Most of the Homeless Cluster's members represent state agencies, while some represent HUD's Columbus office and the Ohio Coalition for the Homeless.

Four factors spurred the development of the Homeless Cluster. First, in 1984 the Ohio Coalition for the Homeless was organized. The coalition advocated for more state funds to be allocated to the growing homeless population, and was instrumental in the creation of the state's Emergency Shelter Program. Also in 1984 the Ohio Department of Mental Health, with the assistance of the National Institute of Mental Health, conducted a study to assess how much of the homeless population consisted of the deinstitutionalized mentally ill. The report was released in 1985 and the governor followed some of its recommendations in naming the Homeless Cluster. Third, the governor had committed himself to the cluster concept for dealing with other state matters. The Homeless Cluster was a logical extension of this idea. Fourth, funding for health care for the homeless, and later for support services for the chronically mentally ill, offered to selected U.S. cities by the Robert Wood Johnson Foundation and the Pew Memorial Trust, served as a catalyst for those interested in this issue.

Because concerns for the mentally ill homeless sparked the formation of the Homeless Cluster, the organization originally focused on mental health issues. By mid-1985 the cluster reported that state agencies were taking several actions to increase access to funds for homeless services, to increase funding for low-income housing, to obtain Robert Wood Johnson/Pew funding for several projects, and to increase the role of community mental health centers. After these initial efforts, activity slowed. However, after the McKinney Act monies became available, the Working Group of the Homeless Cluster was formed and has provided some state-level oversight of the act's activities.

Wisconsin's State Work Group. The need to develop a CHAP for the McKinney Act during the summer of 1987 stimulated the creation of a working group of Wisconsin state agency representatives, city representatives from Milwaukee, Madison, and Racine, providers, and advocates. Since producing the CHAP, members of the working group have met to deal with specific issues of program development. The lead agency expects the working group to continue meeting approximately every six months just to keep in touch. As with all of the other coordinating bodies just described, the group's function is mostly information sharing; it has no authority to request or require agency representatives to do something.

Summary of the State Coordination Efforts

From this review of the structure of state coordination efforts, it is clear that housing agencies are not taking the lead in addressing issues of homelessness. Although the McKinney Act routes the bulk of its financing, which supports various forms of shelter and housing for the homeless, through the federal Department of Housing and Urban Development, the act's funding is most often being managed at the state level by a non-housing agency. This arrangement makes coordination of state efforts and federal resources more difficult, since the primary state agencies are not familiar with HUD programs and grant-making mechanisms, and HUD funders are not familiar with the chief program and policy people at the state level.

This pattern has striking implications. Respondents in all states made it clear that they perceived the problems of the homeless to be broader than the simple need for housing, central as that need might be to the immediate situation leading to homelessness. In each state visited, responsibility for state-level coordination has been placed in the hands of an agency with a broad scope of supportive services and programs: in Ohio, the Department of Mental Health; in all other states visited, a human services/human resources agency. It is also true that the lead agency in each case *wanted* lead agency responsibility and had already shown some leadership in homeless issues.

That in each case the lead agency was not the housing agency indicates the minimal role such agencies commonly play in developing alternatives to homelessness. It also suggests that the problem of homelessness is not being approached from the point of view of prevention.

Development of low-income housing options is certainly one critical link in the long-term solution to homelessness. Logically, this would imply an important role for state housing agencies.

This lack of fit occurs because the usual operations of state housing authorities more closely resemble those of banks than those of most other government agencies. Because they must meet standards of fiscal responsibility to bondholders, housing authorities view different options for developing housing, including housing for the homeless, as investments which must meet a certain level of fiscal safety before the authority will fund them. Proposals for housing in which rents are guaranteed by individual federal benefits to prospective renters, such as Supplemental Security Income (a program for which many disabled homeless are eligible), often are rejected for failure to meet housing authority standards of fiscal safety. The same fate often awaits some of the more creative solutions--such as scattered site apartment housing--being proposed by aspiring developers of housing for the homeless in response to zoning restrictions against congregate housing in certain neighborhoods. Respondents in several states in this study who were providers or individuals who had attempted to develop housing options for the homeless voiced frustration with the conservatism of their state housing finance authority and its funding standards. Clearly they felt that financial support for housing for the homeless would largely have to come from other sources.

Statewide Nongovernment Activities

Most of the states we visited had statewide coalitions or organizations active around issues of homelessness. Often, these were associations of providers such as homeless shelters or domestic violence shelters, but they also included associations of other types of nonprofits and government officials (such as county supervisors).

In California several nongovernment groups have participated in statewide coordination efforts around homelessness. One, the California/Nevada Community Action Association (CAL-NEVA), is a membership organization for providers who receive Community Services Block Grant funds. Its director is the facilitator for the California Working Group for the Homeless. CAL-NEVA has contributed to several reports on the homeless. CAL-NEVA was responsible for writing *Legacy: A Report on the Survey of California Shelters and the Implications for the Nutritional Status of Homeless Children*, funded by the California Department of Economic Opportunity; its director prepared the *Report of the CSAC Homeless Task Force* for the County Supervisors' Association of California (CSAC). Another statewide organization in California is the Coalition for the Homeless, whose members are shelter providers. The coalition sits on the working group, holds an annual meeting of shelter providers and other interested parties, and serves an information-sharing and watchdog role. In addition, the California Alliance Against Domestic Violence, a coalition of domestic violence shelters, has taken a very active role in the state for these shelters, and was a key force in encouraging legislation to support them.

The County Supervisors' Association of California (CSAC) is an active statewide group whose members are local government supervisors. The association has been involved in developing public-private partnerships around homelessness. When county welfare directors brought the severity of the homeless issue to CSAC's Health and Welfare Committee, CSAC appointed a task force to examine the issue. The task force surveyed all counties to find out what they were doing in the area of serving the homeless and prepared a report. The task force was disbanded once the report was published, but may be reappointed to conduct an update. Meanwhile, members of CSAC are working with the Council on Partnerships to develop an on-going group to focus on homeless issues. This council has representatives from public and private sectors, and is co-chaired by the president of CSAC and a vice-president of General Telephone.

In Connecticut the statewide Connecticut Coalition for the Homeless was founded in 1982 by religious leaders who found themselves dealing with mounting requests for emergency shelter. The coalition undertook to address not only the immediate needs of people who are homeless but also the underlying causes of homelessness. From 1982 to 1986 all the coalition's funding came from membership dues and the group worked exclusively through a volunteer board. In 1986 the coalition received funding from the state and hired its first full-time executive director.

The coalition serves as a network for shelter providers. It has successfully fostered a close relationship with the Department of Human Resources, Connecticut's lead agency on homeless issues, and is working to do the same with the Departments of Housing and Mental Health. Coalition members often serve as the liaison between state agency representatives and shelter operators. The coalition has been active in disseminating information directly to the provider community about available funding through the McKinney Act.

Another statewide coalition of providers involved in the homeless issue, the Connecticut Coalition Against Domestic Violence (CCADV), began in 1978, when the state first began to fund domestic violence programs. Until two years ago, the Department of Human Resources was virtually CCADV's sole funder; additional funding sources have now reduced the state's share of CCADV's budget to about half.

It is worth noting that, in Connecticut, a government agency, the Department of Human Resources (DHR), provides partial financial support for the two state coalitions of shelter providers (Connecticut Coalition for the Homeless and Connecticut Coalition Against Domestic Violence). Coalition representatives are also included in program planning and evaluation strategies and cooperate with DHR in developing annual agency budgets around homeless issues. It appears that the working group and DHR have been very successful in promoting cooperative strategies for program development, funding, and operations. It also seems that state financial support has not caused conflicts of interest for the coalitions or co-opted them, but rather has created stable provider organizations that take part in the overall development and coordination of statewide services.

In Georgia two nongovernment coordinating agencies around homelessness have had statewide impact. The statewide coalition is the Georgia Hungry and Homeless Resource Network, a relatively new coalition, with little track record to date. This organization has representatives in 48 cities and towns in Georgia. A steering committee of twelve members meets quarterly to discuss particular issues. The Atlanta Task Force is the voice for the homeless in Georgia, and has had substantial impact on policy. The task force was instrumental in creating the resource network, and is very active, knowledgeable, and well coordinated. It receives funding from the state, and from Fulton and DeKalb counties; state and county officials are members.

The task force has been a strong force in coordinating the activities of service providers in the Atlanta area. It has pulled together coalitions to apply for funding (including from the McKinney Act); suggested and sometimes implemented creative services; and monitored and documented gaps in services, barriers to accessing services by the homeless, and state non-compliance with federal regulations regarding services to the homeless.

In Ohio the primary nongovernment organization working on homeless issues is the Ohio Coalition for the Homeless, mentioned earlier. This Columbus-based organization has a board with representatives from each major city in Ohio as well as various at-large members from other areas. Most board members are homeless advocates or providers. The coalition was formed in 1984 as the result of a conference of providers held in Columbus. At the time there were no federal or state funds available for the homeless, and providers felt it was time to take on a greater advocacy role. The coalition's first activity was to propose and lobby for the legislative action created Ohio's Emergency Shelter Program.

The coalition's role in Ohio is very important. Its director serves on the Ohio Homeless Cluster and has worked with various government agencies at their request to formulate plans for spending McKinney Act and other funds. The coalition wrote the state's CHAP and has taken responsibility for tracking the act's funds (by periodically calling the federal agencies involved in disbursing the monies). In all other states visited these important functions were performed by state agencies. The coalition also undertakes public education activities and offers technical assistance to providers and advice to state agencies. The coalition probably has the best overall view of what is happening in the state with respect to programs for the homeless and has considerable influence in the state both within and outside of government.

It is interesting to note that the three states without statewide coalitions--Georgia, New Mexico and Wisconsin (Georgia officially has a statewide coalition, but it is newly formed and heavily dependent on the Atlanta Task Force)--have one major urban center (Atlanta, Milwaukee,

Albuquerque) in predominantly rural states. Respondents report that, in general, people in these states perceive homelessness to be "only" an Atlanta problem, or an Albuquerque problem, or a Milwaukee problem, and that the rest of the state need not become concerned. This perception may also help to explain why these three states did not have any state agency coordinating council or task force prior to the McKinney Act, why Georgia still does not have a statewide coordinating body in state government, and why funding levels are relatively low in the three states. As will be discussed in the next section, state funding for programs for the homeless in two of these three states (Georgia and New Mexico) is also very low and funding in Wisconsin is somewhat low when compared to the other three states we visited.

STATE FUNDING AND ACTIVITIES

Some of the six states visited by the Institute's staff in 1988 created programs and supported activities to help the homeless several years before the federal McKinney Act. Other states did little or nothing at the state level prior to the act. For some of these latter states the availability of McKinney Act money stimulated the first state-level funding for the homeless, usually to provide the matching funds required by many of the act's programs.

Those states that took early action on their own also tend to outspend available federal resources by a considerable margin. Those states that did not have any state-level programs for the homeless prior to the McKinney Act appear currently to spend more federal than state money on these programs. Table 5.1 shows these patterns in six states during July 1988. These six states were selected because of their geographic representation, participation in national task forces or panels on the homeless, and varied levels of support for programs for the homeless. Selection did not include several states that are doing a great deal for the homeless (such as Massachusetts and New York), and was not designed to highlight only exemplary states. The diversity of programs and activity levels among the six states selected illustrates the wide range of state involvement in homeless issues, from extensive to very little.

As table 5.1 indicates, those states visited that spend the most of their own money in terms of absolute dollars (California and Connecticut) also spend the most per capita, based on 1986 state population. Those that spend the least of their own money (Georgia and New Mexico) also spend the least per capita. The less active states also make less use of federal sources of support other than McKinney Act sources, as indicated by the high proportion of federal money used for the homeless that comes from the act's funds.

Not shown in the table, but evident from interviews with state and local officials, providers in states with more state resources devoted to homeless programs were better able to acquire McKinney Act funds for programs that required matching funds. Because state resources were available, applicants could use them to make their match; applicants from states without extensive state programs and funding sources had more difficulty meeting the match requirements.

Five of the six states visited (excluding New Mexico) have established emergency shelter grants with state funds. Two (California and Ohio) have major state programs for the severely mentally ill homeless. Most have substantial funding for domestic violence shelters, and California supports several other family violence and runaway/homeless youth programs. Connecticut has an extensive array of housing support programs, including security deposit, rent subsidy, "homefinders", case

TABLE 5.1   STATE AND FEDERAL FUNDING FOR HOMELESS PROGRAMS IN SIX STATES

Funding Pattern	California	Connecticut	Georgia	New Mexico	Ohio	Wisconsin
State funds[a] ($s in millions)	$59.8	$43.9	$0.9	$0.2	$5.8	$1.1
State funds expressed as $s per capita of state population	$2.27	$13.83	$0.15	$0.1	$0.54	$0.23
McKinney Act funds[b] ($s in millions)						
To state agencies	$21.1	$2.5	$3.3	$0.5	$ 5.5	$3.5
To non-state agencies[c]	9.2	1.9	2.3	0.8	5.7	1.6
McKinney totals	30.3	4.4	5.	1.3	11.2	5.1
Other federal funds[a] ($s in millions)	$17.4	$6.3	$2.2	$0.1	$0.0	$0.1
State funds as a percentage of (state + McKinney)	66%	91%	13%	12%	34%	18%

Funding Pattern	California	Connecticut	Georgia	New Mexico	Ohio	Wisconsin
McKinney funds as a percentage of all federal funds	63%	41%	72%	97%	100%	98%
McKinney funds to state agencies as a percentage of all McKinney funds in state	70%	56%	60%	37%	49%	70%

Source: Burt and Cohen (1988c), pp. 28-36.

a. State fiscal years 1987-88

b. Federal fiscal year 1987.

c. Non-state agencies may include county and municipal agencies, nonprofit agencies, businesses, labor unions, American Indian tribes, and local Veterans Affairs offices. Eligibility varies by program. Funding data supplied by the Interagency Council for the Homeless, as reported to it by each responsible federal agency.

management, emergency assistance, and other programs. Both California and Connecticut have made serious commitments to increasing the stock of low-income housing through sizeable bonding authority ($120 million in Connecticut; $600 million through two ballot initiatives--Proposition 77 and Proposition 84--in California).

Specific Programs

As states and cities begin to develop programs to serve the homeless, it is important that they have access to information on what has been tried already, and what works. The states visited by the Institute's staff have many outstanding programs that serve the homeless already in place. This section describes some exemplary programs from the states visited, in different program areas such as shelter, housing, food, health, and mental health. We also discuss Connecticut's case management/case coordination program; case management is often mentioned as essential to help homeless people get all the services they need, but in most situations, little case management is actually available. Connecticut's program offers one approach to providing case coordination, accompanied by a reporting system that gives the state information about what services are being used.

Shelter

Shelter is the essential element in the very definition of the homeless state and the primary need of homeless people. This report differentiates shelter from housing. *Shelter* indicates emergency assistance in settings where no one expects people to remain permanently, while *housing* is the development or provision of permanent residences, or the income support necessary to enable very poor people to afford available housing on a permanent basis.

Four of the six states (California, Connecticut, Ohio, and Wisconsin) had legislatively established, state-funded emergency shelter programs in operation before passage of the McKinney Act. These programs provide funds for program operations, and sometimes for minor fix-up and renovations. California created its emergency shelter program in 1983; Connecticut, Ohio, and Wisconsin in 1985. During their latest fiscal year, both California and Connecticut allocated approximately three times as much state money to their emergency shelter programs as their respective states received in McKinney Act emergency shelter grant funding (not counting the act's shelter allocations directly to cities). Ohio's state allocation is about 170 percent of what the state receives from McKinney Act funding, and Wisconsin's state allocation is about equal to its McKinney emergency shelter grant state funding.

Georgia established a state Homeless Shelter Program after the McKinney Act passed, which receives a state allocation equal to approximately one-third of the funding the state receives through McKinney Emergency Shelter Grants. New Mexico does not contribute any state dollars to emergency shelter.

In addition to shelter operating costs, some states have made funds available for site acquisition and major renovation through, for example, the Georgia Residential Finance Authority's Homeless Shelter Revolving Loan Program and the Wisconsin Housing and Economic Development Authority's competitive grant program that uses the authority's unrestricted reserves. California's Emergency Shelter Program required in its first two years that 70 percent of its funding be used for hard costs (acquisition of property, rehabilitation, or leasing of shelters). This distribution was reduced in the third and fourth program years to 60 percent and then to 50 percent. In the most recent funding cycle no hard/soft cost restrictions apply. Connecticut also follows this funding pattern, which may be characterized as "first acquire them and fix them up, then run them."

Some of the states we visited used first Low Income Energy Assistance Block Grant money and then Stripper Well Settlement money to finance one-time weatherization alterations in shelters for the homeless. Other states have also used Stripper Well Settlement money to help the homeless, either for shelter operating costs or for other expenses.[1]

Housing

Many observers see the lack of affordable housing as a key contributor to homelessness. They attribute a great part of the responsibility for this situation to the federal government's virtual withdrawal since 1981 from programs creating low-income housing and its cutback on rental assistance to poor households. Other factors probably contributing to the lack of affordable housing are inflation in the price of housing in some major housing markets, and destruction or conversion of very low rent units (both apartments and single room occupancy dwellings).

In many cities the gap between the incomes of poor people and the price of housing is wide, and getting wider. For example, the General Accounting Office (1987, p. 10) estimates that in 1983, 30 percent of the nation's low-income households paid over 70 percent of their income for housing. This percentage by far exceeds HUD's standard of affordability (that 30 percent of a household's income goes for housing). In light of these facts, state activities to increase the availability of affordable housing are clearly critical in the effort to get the homeless back into housing and ultimately to prevent homelessness.

Several of the states we visited had a number of innovative and ambitious programs to get homeless people back into permanent housing, and to encourage the development of more affordable housing throughout the state. Some programs assist currently homeless individuals to locate and pay for existing housing. Some provide housing plus support services for specific subgroups of the homeless population (such as people with AIDS). Some states are developing special projects for homeless or transitional occupants. In some states massive bonding authority has been obtained to expand low-income housing for all people in the state.

Assisting Currently Homeless People into Permanent Housing. Connecticut has a number of programs that help currently homeless people find and afford permanent housing. Its Rental Assistance Program (RAP), run by the Department of Housing, provides rent subsidies to low-income persons or families. Participants must earn 60 percent or less of the area's median income, and 30 percent of their adjusted monthly income must go to rent and utilities, with RAP paying the difference. This program is currently funded at $8 million per year, with 90 percent going to homeless families. Funds are administered by the Department of Housing directly or are given to municipalities where local agents such as CAP agencies or housing authorities are responsible for distributing the funds.

Connecticut began funding a second rent subsidy program through the Department of Income Maintenance in April 1989. If a family is not receiving Section 8 or state housing subsidies and it is paying rent equal to 50 percent or more of household income, the family will be eligible for a $50/month subsidy. The program is expected to cover 18,000-19,000 eligible cases.

Since October 1986, Connecticut has funded a Security Deposit Program, managed by the Department of Human

Resources, that has been second only to the rental assistance funds in its ability to place homeless families in permanent housing. Under the program the state may pay a security deposit totalling up to two months' rent directly to a landlord. Should the family move in less than two months, the landlord must repay the remaining balance to the Commissioner of Human Resources, and the family remains entitled to have that balance paid on its behalf to another landlord. Since the program's inception, security deposits have helped place nearly 2,000 families in permanent housing.

Connecticut's Homefinders Program began in New Haven during the summer of 1986 as a pilot project in response to an especially high need at the time. The New Haven community organized to bring attention to great numbers of homeless families living in hotels and motels, and in response, the state developed the Homefinders Program. A team of three people was hired to find housing and to negotiate rents for the homeless families. Part of the task was to convince landlords that they would be taking no extraordinary risks in renting to these families. The departments of Income Maintenance, Human Resources, and Housing joined forces, allocating $300,000 in 1986 to provide some rental assistance subsidies. The money was sufficient to place 40 families. The program was subsequently expanded, and to date 300 families have been relocated. Of these, 280 received state subsidies, while the rest were eligible for Section 8 subsidies. The pilot project also demonstrated that having workers specifically assigned to find housing frees the case coordinators to give appropriate time and attention to the other needs of the homeless families.

Housing for Homeless Persons with AIDS or ARC. In California, San Francisco has embarked on a unique program to provide housing, along with support services, to homeless persons with Acquired Immune Deficiency Syndrome (AIDS) or AIDS Related Complex (ARC). It is estimated that in San Francisco 400-600 homeless persons, or approximately 10 percent of the city's homeless population, have AIDS or ARC. Called Single Room Occupancy Residence for Homeless Persons with AIDS or AIDS Related Complex, the program serves many such people who are recovering from dependencies on illegal drugs.

The program is sponsored by Catholic Charities of San Francisco County. It started serving clients in March 1987 out of a hotel located south of Market Street. Because of problems with that property, the program began to look for other options, and is now planning to renovate a two-story, 11,000-square-foot building into 32 single occupancy residences to provide long-term housing for their clients. The program raised $1.7 million for the purchase and renovation of the building. Operating funds will come from HUD Section 8 certificates. The program combined various sources of funding, including Catholic Charities, the Mayor's Office of Housing and Economic Development (through its Community Housing Rehabilitation Loan Fund), HUD's Section 8 Moderate Rehabilitation Program, the Savings Associations Mortgage Company, an anonymous private donor, the MacCauley Foundation, and the McKinney Act SRO Moderate Rehabilitation program. Catholic Charities provides on-site case management, counseling, and 24-hour support services and supervision. Connecticut also has a program for housing and support services for persons with AIDS and ARC. Bonding funds totalling $1.6 million and operating funds of $150,000 have been authorized by the legislature.

Development of Special Projects for Homeless or Transitional Occupants. The Housing for the Homeless Program in Connecticut provides grants-in-aid to community housing development corporations, municipal developers, or nonprofit corporations. Funds can assist with the cost of property acquisition, building construction, or building rehabilitation. Eligible projects include rooming houses for homeless people or multi-family dwellings for persons or families in need of transitional housing and support services. The project began in 1985 as a pilot program. Funding has equalled almost $8 million through 1987, with an additional $7 million committed for 1988. Connecticut has also appropriated funds that the Department of Human Resources can use for grants to cover operating and social services costs for transitional housing facilities, whether these facilities have been constructed with state funds or with grants under the McKinney Act. This flexibility is one example of Connecticut's effort to establish effective program linkages between housing and social services.

Bonding Authority and Other Mechanisms to Expand Low-income Housing. In FY 1987-88, as a component of its strategy to combat homelessness, Connecticut authorized $100 million in bonding authority to the Department of Housing to promote the development of low-income housing. These funds support several different programs, including the Housing for the Homeless Program, and others that fund the development of mutual housing, limited equity cooperatives, urban homesteading, and elderly and congregate housing. In addition, the state funds other community development and site acquisition/site development programs which have included emergency shelters.

Connecticut also has a PRIME program (Private Rental Investment Mortgage and Equity) that provides low-interest mortgages from the Department of Housing and the Connecticut Housing Finance Agency to promote construction of mixed income, multi-family housing in the private sector. Projects must be 25 units, with 20-40 percent of the units rented to persons with incomes less than 50 percent of the area median.

The Connecticut Housing Partnership Program was developed by the Department of Housing to encourage communities to develop housing for the low- and moderate-income population. Through this program interested municipalities set up a local housing partnership, which includes the chief elected official, members of housing and development agencies, public interest groups, and local urban planning and land development professionals. The Department of Housing then helps the partnership develop a local housing strategy, identify resources, and provide information on housing programs and finances. Once the municipality initiates an activity, the Department of Housing gives it priority funding. Municipalities that participate also receive primary consideration from the Department of Environmental Protection for open space and water quality projects (sewage and land use). Once the housing activity is completed and there is evidence of ongoing activity to develop affordable housing, the Department of Transportation will increase the town grant for roads by 25 percent for that year and the three subsequent years. This project has not yet been fully implemented in Connecticut, but has been successful in Massachusetts. A major difference between the two programs is that in Massachusetts, specific money was allocated for these programs, while in Connecticut programs receive priority for use of general funds.

In California voters passed Proposition 77 in June 1988. Advocates describe this as a major victory, even though the proposition was not directly targeted at the homeless. The measure provides $150 million in general obligation bond financing for the rehabilitation of low-income housing. Another initiative, Proposition 84, was approved by voters in November 1988. Proposition 84 is a $450 million housing and homeless bond measure that provides financing for emergency shelter for the homeless, rental housing for the elderly and the handicapped, and homeownership assistance to working families. It includes $35 million to rehabilitate 33,000 new beds for the homeless in emergency shelters; $40 million to rehabilitate 22,000 residential hotel units; $15 million for a new Family Housing Demonstration Program that will produce 900 units of housing designed for single- and working-parent families; and $10 million for farm labor centers to produce 300 units of family housing for migrant farm workers.

Food Programs. Food is second only to shelter among the emergency needs of the homeless. We heard of no special food programs initiated from the state level in the states we visited, although Connecticut does provide financial support for the warehousing and distribution system that supplies food to soup kitchens, shelters, and food banks. The McKinney Act becomes involved in food programs through its extension for one more year of the Temporary Emergency Food Assistance Program (TEFAP), and its authorization of the Emergency Food and Shelter Program (known widely as FEMA for the Federal Emergency Management Administration through which its money flows). Congress had funded both TEFAP and the EFSP through successive rounds of temporary appropriations--TEFAP since 1981 and the EFSP since 1983. Although evaluations of these programs indicate that they do meet the goals set for them (Food and Nutrition Service 1987; Burt and Burbridge 1985), neither program is directed to the special needs of the homeless.

Health

Most studies of the homeless show that they experience significant chronic and acute health problems, but often do not get the health care they need. After shelter and food, many who work with the homeless see health care as the next most critical need. Despite the need, however, the homeless may have a difficult time using regular medical providers; certainly they do not use medical care appropriately, following the pattern of many poor people in overusing emergency rooms.

A number of years ago there was some debate as to whether homeless people would use even specially designed health services that met them where they were most likely to be--in or near soup kitchens and shelters, or actually on the streets. During the last few years exemplary programs providing health care for the homeless have been established, many through funding from the Robert Wood Johnson Foundation. These programs clearly demonstrate the need for health care among the homeless, the willingness of homeless people to use these services, and the ability that exists to design programs that reach and treat this population.

In four of the six states we visited, the city we had selected for focused attention had received a Robert Wood Johnson Health Care for the Homeless grant: San Francisco, Albuquerque, Cleveland and Milwaukee. Most projects were in their third year of this funding; all had applied for and received McKinney Act Primary Health Services grants to continue and expand their services. We met with representatives of three of these four projects, and describe two at length here.

The Cleveland Health Care for the Homeless Project sponsors the Downtown Drop-in Center, which is both a clinic and a center where homeless individuals can spend the day. It operates six days a week, Monday through Saturday, opening at 8:30 a.m., the time when most night shelters close. It provides the following services:

✦ a day shelter where homeless individuals can congregate secure from the threat of violence on the streets;

✦ primary health care facilities--screening, referral, and on-site physician care;

✦ respite care--bed rest during the day to support the recuperation of 12 to 15 ill or injured clients;

✦ nursing care--dressing changes, foot soaks, and inhalation therapy;

✦ employment counseling and referral to local employment and training services;

✦ substance abuse counseling, including drug and alcohol recovery programs;

✦ case management--professional social work resources for developing individual strategies for finding housing and employment;

✦ mental health counseling;

✦ information and referral--connecting the client to other agencies that can assist them; and,

✦ rest rooms.

The Milwaukee Health Care for the Homeless Program offers similar services through its Robert Wood Johnson Foundation funding and is using McKinney Act money to:

✦ expand hours of coverage by doctors and nurses at the six Robert Wood Johnson shelter and soup kitchen clinic sites, and offer new coverage to battered women's shelters and one more meal site;

✦ obtain a computer and a medical data entry staff person to make recordkeeping more consistent and to support better health care;

✦ care for the chronically mentally ill homeless population--support one full-time community support worker, one full-time money manager for chronically mentally ill clients, and two psychiatrists (one in shelters and meal sites, and the other, along with a full-time nurse-practitioner, to walk the streets, identify and assess long-term chronically mentally ill individuals);

✦ care for the chemically dependent homeless population--support two money managers to help people obtain housing and benefits, and to stabilize them in this placement, and one full-time street worker to locate individuals and bring them in for care;

✦ double the general street outreach of the project, from two male street workers supported with several small grants, to four by adding two female street workers. The result of adding women street workers has been the ability to identify and assist more homeless families living in abandoned buildings and other situations. Street work is now available 12 hours a day, six and one-half days a week;

✦ operate a support group for people the project has assisted to help them get permanent housing;

✦ operate an outreach van, which has encountered 1,100-1,200 individuals so far, and placed 100 in permanent housing; and,

✦ provide continuing education and training for employees.

In Connecticut the only pre-McKinney Act health care program run specifically for the homeless is in Hartford. The University of Hartford is using support from the state Department of Human Resources and the U.S. Department of Education's Fund for the Improvement of Post-Secondary Education to provide tuition reimbursement to registered nurses who have returned to school to get their college degree. In exchange, each nurse spends eight hours a week doing nursing care in Hartford shelters, as the practicum part of a required community health course. In the shelters the nurses provide treatment for lice, scabies, trauma, food problems, and sexually transmitted diseases. They do drug and alcohol abuse educational programs, and assessments of other physical problems, for which they provide either treatment or referrals. In women's and family shelters they do a good deal of education and referral for family planning issues.

Mental Health

Mental health problems are quite prevalent among the homeless. Many homeless persons have a history of institutionalization in mental hospitals. Others, particularly younger persons, are diagnosably mentally ill (and often also chemically dependent) but, because far fewer people are hospitalized today than would have been hospitalized 15 or 20 years ago, they have never spent time in a mental hospital. In addition, many homeless persons are depressed and demoralized enough to need clinical treatment, whether or not they would be diagnosed as having a major mental illness.

Different surveys have shown different proportions of the homeless population who might be considered chronically mentally ill--ranging from about 20 percent up to 40-50 percent. Many have multiple problems, including chemical dependency along with mental illness. However, sometimes the acknowledgment that many homeless people have mental or emotional problems has been overgeneralized into a perception that homelessness is *almost entirely* a problem of the chronically mentally ill. Respondents in two of the states visited, California and Ohio, while applauding the extensive efforts of their mental health systems in extending services for the chronically mentally ill, nevertheless voiced some distress that the greatest amount of attention in their states has been directed toward the chronically mentally ill homeless, with comparatively less effort going toward helping the homeless with other problems.

In recent years, partly as a result of the numbers of homeless persons on the streets, the nation has come to recognize that the emptying of state mental hospitals since 1965 has not been accompanied by a parallel development of community-based services for the chronically mentally ill. This lack exists despite the fact that federal legislation originally promised such development (Community Mental Health Centers Construction Act of 1963 and subsequent CMHC legislation). Some communities and states have begun to fill this gap. Two states we visited, California and Ohio, have recently developed very extensive state-supported programs for the mentally ill homeless.

In California the Community Support System for Homeless Mentally Disabled Persons was established in September 1985. The state Department of Mental Health estimated that California has between 75,000 and 90,000 homeless persons, up to 35 percent of whom have some form of mental disorder (about 35,000 mentally disabled homeless). The Department of Mental Health's activities on behalf of the homeless started in FY 1985-86 with $20 million for the provision of services to the chronically mentally disabled homeless. In 1986-87 and 1987-88, the state allocated $20.2 million for the homeless mentally disabled (known in California as the HMD). The same amount is proposed for 1988-89.

These funds are used for the homeless as well as for persons at risk of becoming homeless. The state allocates funds to local mental health programs, which provide services to the homeless either directly or through contracts with the private sector. In addition to mental health services, these funds can be used for community support services such as food, shelter, housing search assistance, medical and dental care, and transportation. Some county programs are developing continuum of care programs which attempt to address the multiple needs of mentally disabled homeless people.

In Ohio the Department of Mental Health has long been active in developing services for the homeless or those at risk of becoming homeless. In addition to special state appropriations for housing the chronically mentally ill, the department has committed considerable amounts from its operating and capital budgets to activities that benefit this group. It has provided $2.5 million in operating funds to the Robert Wood Johnson Community Support Programs for the Chronically Mentally Ill in Cincinnati, Columbus, and Toledo, and $5 million from its capital account to these projects. Although not exclusively for the homeless, these programs especially target the chronically mentally ill who are homeless or who are at risk of becoming so. Technically, the $5 million is a loan fund to be used by nonprofit development corporations in these sites to leverage other money for permanent housing. But the loan will be forgiven in 40 years if the same client population is being served. The department has also committed $1 million to its Money and Mailboxes project in Cleveland in the form of a loan to leverage funds for permanent housing for the homeless. Money and Mailboxes is similar to the three Robert Wood Johnson programs.

The extent of Ohio's commitment illustrates the clear acknowledgment of the Ohio Department of Mental Health that permanent housing, supported by services, is a critical need for the mentally ill, many of whom are either homeless or potentially homeless. The department opposes transitional housing--such as group homes--that unnecessarily segregate and stigmatize mental health clients. Further, under the group home concept, housing is viewed as a service that a client receives when his or her mental illness is in an acute phase, and not otherwise. Instead the department believes that the mentally ill should have access to their own housing, where they should be able to remain even when they no longer require immediate services from the mental health system. Department policy would integrate the mentally ill with non-mental health clients as well. Thus out of a two-year, $22 million capital budget that once was used primarily for group homes and emergency crisis centers, the Ohio Department of Mental Health has committed $11 million for permanent housing projects. The dollars are intended to leverage other funds for permanent, low-income housing that would house clients who do and do not suffer from mental illnesses. Although not specifically for the homeless, this funding source has great potential to serve this population.

The Department of Mental Health has encountered several obstacles in spending these funds, however. A major barrier to program development in Ohio is a constitutional provision prohibiting the state from lending funds for housing (Wisconsin has a similar prohibition). Thus the state cannot go directly into the low-income housing business; it can only give grants to nonprofit agencies which, in turn, can set up loan programs. This prohibition has caused problems because the department wants to use its capital funds to encourage low-income housing, but cannot lend the money directly for housing. Nor can its money be used for the non-mentally ill. Nor can the department join in partnerships with private for-profit developers. This leaves only nonprofit development corporations, many of which are reluctant to engage in developing housing for the mentally ill, particularly if department clients are to be integrated with non-mentally ill persons. In some cases, the department has had to encourage the development of new nonprofit housing corporations in order to carry out its goals.

Case Management/Case Coordination

Many respondents voiced strong beliefs that case management was needed to help homeless people get all the necessary services, and for follow-up to see that the services were effective. They were equally sure that, in most places, case management did not exist. However, one state we visited, Connecticut, has made a significant commitment to providing coordinated case management for homeless clients.

In Connecticut the state Department of Human Resources funds case coordinators in most shelters, provides clear job descriptions for these workers, and uses a reporting/tracking system. Recognizing that emergency shelter was just the first step in preventing homelessness, the Governor's Task Force on the Homeless, discussed earlier, strongly recommended that the state provide supportive services to shelter clients in order to enable them to obtain permanent housing and become self-sufficient. Case coordinators concentrate their services during the period of homelessness, but also carryout follow-up services. A task force of government and provider representatives led by the Department of Human Resources is currently developing an evaluation system for case coordination, which will include follow-up contacts to determine the stability and income sources of formerly homeless individuals who had received assistance to obtain permanent housing.

Funding for case coordination was first provided in 1986-87, during which 27 shelter facilities (out of 40) employed full- or part-time case coordinators. This number expanded to 32 shelters in state fiscal year (SFY) 1987-88. The state has set a goal of supplying one coordinator for every 25 adult shelter clients, and will be close to meeting that goal with SFY 1988-89 funding. Services provided by or arranged for by coordinators include child care, transportation, job search assistance, housing search assistance, a security deposit program, and support in applying for various forms of public assistance and social service programs. Case coordinators gave supportive services to 16,299 people in SFY 1986-87. Follow-up services (after entering permanent housing) were provided to 1,761 people within 30 days, 1,271 people within 60 days, and 1,869 people within 120 days.

Connecticut also funds outreach, assessment, and case management services for the homeless chronically mentally ill through its Department of Mental Health. Both outreach/assessment and case management staff are housed at community mental health centers. In theory, the outreach/assessment person visits shelters to assess the mental health status of shelter residents who have been identified by shelter operators as in potential need of mental health services. If the outreach worker deems it appropriate, a mental health case manager is assigned to the case. Ideally the assignment of a mental health case manager would relieve the DHR-funded case coordinator of all case coordination responsibilities, and the resident would be transferred to the mental health case manager for all service needs (not just mental health). In practice the relationships among the outreach/assessment person, the mental health case manager, and the shelter-based case coordinator are still being worked out in most facilities.

ISSUES IN THE DEVELOPMENT OF SERVICES

Duplication of Services

A routine concern of Congress when providing federal funds for a new program area is that these funds should not be used to supplant local or state funds, and that they should not be used to provide services that are already available. However, no one interviewed in any of the states we visited was seriously concerned about duplication of services for the homeless. Generally, respondents felt that the need was so great that even if two separate but identical programs were funded, they would encounter more than enough homeless people to serve. The only voice of even minor dissent to this position came from a Connecticut state official who felt that, because federal agencies other than HUD did not require applicants for McKinney Act money to submit either state or local CHAPs, they sometimes funded a program in a locality in which a similar state-funded program already existed, while another locality had no such service. This respondent was concerned about fairness in the allocation of federal resources, not that the new program would be superfluous.

Needed Services, Service Gaps

Low-income Housing. Everyone interviewed agreed that the basic service gap creating homelessness was the lack of affordable low-income housing. Everyone blamed weakness of federal policy for this circumstance, including withdrawal of supports to create more low-income housing and cuts in rental subsidies. Local respondents were unanimous and vociferous; state-level people were equally unanimous, especially about the withdrawal of the federal government from the housing business and its effects. State officials in non-housing agencies spoke as clearly as local service providers about the need for their state to take steps to create more low-income housing. Housing authorities and legislative representatives were in substantial agreement but were somewhat less adamant--perhaps because they actually have to come up with the money and the programs to make it happen.

Respondents were somewhat less clear about the appropriate mechanisms for creating affordable housing. New construction, renovation, and subsidies were all advocated, and all are being tried to some degree. However, all providers and many state officials maintained that the current system of emergency shelter care was merely patching a crumbling structure, and could not compensate for the basic lack of affordable housing.

Several respondents mentioned the issue of single resident occupancy housing as a necessary element in the overall creation of more affordable housing. Until recently both states and the federal government have tended to resist funding physical renovation or subsidizing rents for this type of housing, which is nevertheless perceived by most respondents as the most reasonable approach to speedy affordable housing for many disabled homeless persons.

Only Connecticut among the six states visited had a clear, state-level policy commitment and a plan for dealing with preventing homelessness through the development of low-income housing, as well as supplying interim band-aids in the form of emergency services. However, even in Connecticut, the Coalition for the Homeless argued that the state legislature has refused to create the mechanisms for state overrides of local zoning and other restrictive ordinances. The state has chosen to deal with municipalities through a range of incentive programs (described earlier), rather than through coercive approaches.

Permanent Affordable Housing with Support Services. Interviewees saw certain segments of the homeless population as requiring long-term (often lifelong) assistance with meeting housing costs, and also some level of ongoing supportive services. The chronically mentally ill and the chronic substance abuser were usually mentioned as two (overlapping) groups of homeless with long-term inabilities to provide for themselves. Supportive services need not be live-in; considerable success has been achieved by several programs we visited (notably the Health Care for the Homeless projects in Milwaukee and Cleveland) with money management arrangements as the basic supportive activity once clients get SSI or other benefits, with service coordination supplied as needed. Some respondents also mentioned long-term sober living facilities for recovering substance abusers.

Homeless women were a third segment of the homeless population in need of supportive services coupled with housing. Specifically, some respondents noted that some homeless women with children were afraid to seek services for fear their children would be taken away from them--either because of their homelessness *per se*, or because they had additional problems with either mental illness, chemical dependency, or both. Other respondents noted the needs of women who had suffered multiple types of physical and sexual abuse, including repeated abusive relationships as adults, to receive supportive services in a transitional living situation providing housing for up to two years.

Emergency Service Gaps. Respondents identified the following gaps in emergency services:

✦ Case management or case coordination for currently homeless persons is needed to enable clients to access the services and benefits which they need or to which they are entitled. As noted previously, only Connecticut has made a serious commitment to supply case coordination services to all sheltered persons. Case management in the other states visited is described as spotty to non-existent.

✦ Health care is seen as another serious gap, especially in localities without a Health Care for the Homeless program. These programs now have established a sufficient track record to demonstrate how much can be done to deliver health care to the homeless. The have developed numerous techniques for actually reaching homeless people who need health care. "We don't know if this will work" should no longer be a viable excuse for failure to support health care programs for homeless persons.

✦ Lack of transportation is often mentioned as a service gap that affects many aspects of being homeless. Lack of transportation (among other things) keeps homeless children from attending school, keeps homeless persons from reaching needed services or offices where they can apply for benefits, and keeps homeless adults from access to jobs.

✦ Services for homeless children, from day care to Head Start to public school education to mental health care, are an acknowledged gap everywhere. Dually diagnosed persons (mental illness and chemical dependency) and homeless or near-homeless youth (including foster care children who are "aging out" of the care system) are also frequently mentioned as groups in the homeless population who do not fit neatly into a category and therefore are often refused services. A number of respondents in California pointed out that it was shortsighted to fail to help the homeless youth of today, who could become the difficult-to-serve homeless adults of tomorrow. This perception is supported by data from a recent Minneapolis study (Piliavin, et al. 1987) that indicated more than one-third of the homeless had spent some time in foster care--a much higher proportion than for the general public.

Gaps in Preventive Factors. In addition to the universal agreement that lack of affordable housing contributes to homelessness, respondents cited several other factors that may be construed as service gaps. Most of the issues covered here pertained to the disjuncture between housing costs and disposable income, and represented different ways of closing this gap. Inadequate levels of public benefits (AFDC, GA, housing benefits, SSI, food stamps) were often mentioned, and may represent the income side of the affordable housing dilemma. Educational and job skills deficits were often mentioned as reasons why many homeless cannot become self-sufficient. Respondents believed that remedial efforts were necessary for those currently homeless, but equally important were similar services to assist people vulnerable to homelessness with literacy and job skills so they could make an adequate living. In the same context, respondents suggested increases in the minimum wage to levels that made housing affordable.

A somewhat different focus was the recognition that most programs for the homeless were funded in ways that prohibited them from serving persons and households living "doubled-up" with other households and other near-homeless people. Yet respondents believed that if they could help such people obtain needed benefits or meet other needs, they could prevent additional cases of homelessness.

Barriers to Service Receipt

The difficulties in the process of applying for public benefits were mentioned in every state as barriers to service receipt, although many examples given pertained to specific benefit programs. Homeless persons with case coordinators were generally perceived to fare much better at getting benefits than those who were left to try on their own. A recent California study (Vernez et al. 1988) documented that, in the counties studied, only two out of five homeless persons eligible for SSI received these benefits. The advantages of having a case manager can be seen when one compares this to the situation in Connecticut, where the Department of Mental Health estimates that approximately 90-95 percent of its chronically mentally ill clients receive SSI, or in Wisconsin where the Department of Health and Social Services says that most of the chronic alcoholics known to the department are SSI recipients.

Respondents mentioned several common application difficulties, such as lack of information about programs, lack of outreach, difficult and confusing application forms, long waiting times, and office locations inconvenient to shelters. But the biggest problem with applications for the homeless is assembling and hanging onto the necessary documentation. Required documents can include birth certificates, picture identification cards, and proof of residency--all quite difficult for the homeless to produce, for different reasons.

Homeless people also continue to encounter problems accessing benefit programs because of a lack of a fixed address. This has been a problem with food stamps (despite repeated policy clarifications from the federal level) and with the Supplemental Feeding Program for Women, Infants, and Children (WIC). A number of Ohio officials mentioned that homeless persons were unable to receive WIC benefits because they did not have an appropriate address and administrators of the WIC program in Ohio did not accept shelter addresses. The Ohio Coalition for the Homeless brought this problem to the attention of the Department of Health which, in conjunction with the Department of Human Services, has removed this barrier; WIC recipients in Ohio are no longer required to have a permanent home address.

Residency and the lack of a fixed address present particular problems for homeless children who need to enroll in school. In all states visited except Wisconsin, school residency requirements form a major barrier to the enrollment of homeless children. In contrast, Wisconsin state law requires any school district to serve any child residing, however temporarily, within its borders. In exchange, the state contributes substantial equalization payments to help less wealthy districts provide equal education across the state.

Federal SSI administrative practices earlier in this decade resulted in large numbers of mentally disabled individuals being terminated from the SSI/Social Security Disability Insurance (SSDI) rolls and increased the difficulty of obtaining an initial determination of eligibility. Respondents in several states said these practices had created a serious barrier to service receipt for many extremely vulnerable individuals, some of whom subsequently became homeless.

Some providers cited the personal problems of homeless individuals, including drug and alcohol abuse, as barriers to their receiving services. Others noted a pattern of going on and then off benefit programs due to an inability to follow through on required recertification procedures. Some programs have solved these problems even for heavy substance abusers with a combination of benefits determination, housing placement, and money management (appointing a money manager to receive the benefits, pay the rent and other bills, and give the client the remainder in small installments), so that previously homeless persons become housed in stable circumstances and remain so.

Barriers to Program Development Specific to the McKinney Act

Many people in every state mentioned specific problems with the McKinney Act, although they also said they were very happy to have both the money and the federal recognition of the problem that the act implies. Specific problems fell into two categories--substantive and procedural.

The dominant substantive difficulty with the McKinney Act, in the perceptions of all state and local people, was its heavy focus on bricks and mortar for emergency shelters, its extremely limited provisions for operating costs and staffing, and its relative lack of focus on serious prevention efforts. As to the latter, the general feeling could be characterized as, "It's nice to have it, but it can't compensate for the lack of low-income housing." Respondents noted the irony that in order to receive a McKinney Act shelter grant, HUD requires a provider to continue operating that shelter for 10 years, yet the act provides no money to pay for the costs of actually running the shelter, only money for physically rehabilitating the building that will house the shelter.

A disjuncture exists in the act between programs that pay for bricks and mortar and funding for other program elements (staffing, maintenance costs, special services); most of the procedural criticism of the act stemmed from this circumstance. State-level people felt they had a difficult time planning a comprehensive approach to homelessness based on McKinney Act programs because they could not be sure that funding would actually be available for key elements of any plan they devised.

This same complaint was frequently voiced by providers as well. Many local people spoke of the difficulties of putting together a program under the McKinney Act, when you had to get your building from one grant program, your staff from another, your operating expenses from a third, each controlled by a different federal agency with whom you may have not previously dealt, from whom you had no assurance of funding, and from whom both requests for proposals (RFPs) and funding arrived on unpredictable schedules (proposals being due too soon after an RFP came out and money not coming through soon enough).

Not only was it difficult within the McKinney Act constraints to put together a comprehensive program plan, but the application process was often described as excruciating. RFP release dates were too closely spaced, and many providers spoke of "proposal burnout" from having to write one proposal after another. They also mentioned that most provider agencies lack administrative staff to write proposals.

Specific problems with HUD restrictions on the Permanent Housing for Handicapped Homeless Persons and Transitional Housing for the Homeless programs were mentioned repeatedly. These problems were:

✦ *Unrealistic turnaround time.* The turnaround time between issuing the RFP and requiring a response was too short for any applicant that did not already have a deal practically signed, sealed, and delivered to put together a viable program and obtain the required signoffs. Although HUD was informed of this, and indeed had to issue a second round of the RFP because they did not receive enough applicants the first time ($5 million in applications for $30 million in funds), HUD made the turnaround time for the second round even shorter.

✦ *Site control problems.* HUD insisted that an applicant assure access to the proposed program site during the entire application process, which could be as long as six months. Few landlords are willing to hold a building for that long with no assurance *from HUD* that the program will ultimately be approved. If an applicant did not already *own* the building in question, the applicant had to risk its own money in whatever type of guarantee the landlord was willing to accept. Few applicants could work out this type of arrangement, especially on short notice.

✦ *No displacement problems.* HUD required that no building could be used for these programs if anyone who lived there would be displaced by the conversion to program use. In cities with many vacant properties that could be condemned or foreclosed on and turned into program sites this posed no problems. But in many places building that were 75-90 percent empty, with eager landlords, had to be passed up because of the "no displacement" rule. A number of subterfuges were developed by applicants to get around this, but some providers felt there was no way to be honest and apply, and chose not to apply.

Finally, we heard a good deal of evidence that prospective applicants often could not generate the required matching funds. Granted that part of the McKinney Act rationale was to use federal funding to stimulate states to further action, we cannot assume that no need exists in a state just because state level decisionmakers, including legislators, refuse to appropriate or allocate match money. Numerous state-local barriers to program development, discussed later, attest to the difficulties potential providers face in finding matching funds from state and local governments, independent of the needs of the homeless people who come to them for help.

Respondents also expressed concern that federal officials might conclude no need existed for specific services--most often mentioned were transitional and permanent housing--because HUD had received few applications despite giving potential providers two chances. Respondents insisted that the restrictions accompanying the funding made it practically impossible to obtain, even though many communities sorely need these programs.

One strong preference voiced by state and local respondents alike was that Congress put the entire amount of federal funds into a block grant, to be used for services for the homeless according to the best judgments of states and localities. Respondents pointed out that needed services and programs shift quickly at the local level as certain basic needs are met and providers move on to tackle the harder problems of long-term solutions. They argued that congressional processes are too slow and federal laws are too cumbersome to respond with sufficient flexibility to the different needs of jurisdictions at very different points in the development of services for the homeless.

Demands of Developing the Comprehensive Homeless Assistance Plan Required by the McKinney Act

The McKinney Act required states (and certain other designated jurisdictions) to prepare a CHAP and have it approved by the Department of Housing and Urban Development before the state could receive any money through McKinney Act programs. Ideally the process of developing the CHAP could serve as a coordinating and planning mechanism, enabling states to create a blueprint for initial and ongoing program development for the homeless. In many people's opinions, the CHAP should also have served a guidance function for *federal* agencies, showing them the types of services and geographical locations that states had already covered and giving a picture of where additional support would be most valuable. To some extent the opportunity for the CHAP to serve the former function has not materialized; the second function has been even less in evidence.

In five of the six states visited, a state agency took the lead in developing the CHAP (in Ohio the Ohio Coalition for the Homeless wrote the CHAP):

State	Lead Agency	Coordinating Group
California	Health and Welfare Agency	Task Force
Connecticut	Department of Human Resources	State Work Group
Georgia	Georgia Residential Finance Agency	none
New Mexico	Department of Human Services	M c K i n n e y Task Force
Wisconsin	Department of Health and Social Services, Bureau of Community Services	State Work Group

In two of these states, New Mexico and Wisconsin, no state-level coordinating group existed prior to the McKinney Act, and the requirement to produce a CHAP stimulated these states to form their first coordinating group. In two other states, Ohio and California, significant organizing at the state level with the participation of state agencies had occurred prior to the act, but respondents felt that it gave further impetus to serious planning and coordination.

Despite the work that went into developing the CHAP, quite a number of respondents in different states felt that the CHAP was *not* serving the function of a blueprint for their state. Several reasons were given, depending partly on the position and responsibilities of the speaker. They fell into three broad categories: (1) no teeth, (2) incomplete information, and (3) funding uncertainty.

No Teeth. A number of respondents said that their state's CHAP did a reasonable job of identifying service gaps and needs, but that the CHAP process contained no schedule beyond the date of submission of the CHAP, no requirement that states pursue plans to fill the identified gaps, and no leverage should proposed plans fail to materialize. Obviously states have not chosen to give any power to their coordinating groups and task forces, so no penalty follows if plans are not carried out, or if proposed efforts to develop programs are left incomplete. Respondents outside of state government made this complaint most commonly, but a few government employees also voiced it.

Incomplete Information. State agency representatives, especially those from the lead agency, expressed considerable dissatisfaction with the way the McKinney Act set up the CHAP process for designated cities. The act required cities of a certain size to submit their own CHAPs, but did not require them to share their CHAPs with the task forces working on the state CHAP. This resulted in gaps in the state CHAPs, and a reduced ability of state agencies to plan where they would allocate state monies for the homeless, since they did not know what additional resources cities might be receiving from McKinney Act funds.

A further difficulty in planning at the state level arises because not all of the McKinney Act funds flow through state agencies. A state coordinating group cannot plan comprehensively when certain key elements in the plan will be funded directly by the federal government to local governments and private providers if they apply and their applications are approved. If a state is not providing direct funding or matching funds, the state agency may often not know who is applying and who has received funding for specific programs. Certainly, the state agencies cannot *direct* local governments and private providers to apply for the funds for which only they are eligible; therefore some state agency representatives felt they could not plan adequately for the services that these funds might support.

Funding Uncertainty. McKinney Act funding is divided into many programs; some are distributed by formula with no match, some by formula with matching requirements, and some through competitive grant programs at the national level (also with matching requirements). Almost all respondents, regardless of position as government or private representatives, agreed that it was extremely difficult to piece together a comprehensive program under the McKinney Act. Support for purchase and renovation of buildings comes from one program; funds for operating cost (which are not even close to adequate) come from another. Funds for staffing come from yet another program and are also limited; funds for special but necessary services such as health care, mental health care, chemical dependency treatment, or job training come from still others. Separate programs within the act are only available to certain special categories of applicants. While respondents are grateful to have some federal money available, they almost unanimously prefer a block grant approach that truly lets local decisionmakers allocate the total funding available in a more coherent manner.

Finally, there is the issue of what use federal agencies made of the CHAPs. Respondents in most states came to feel that the CHAPs were from the outset a meaningless bureaucratic hurdle, that federal agencies did not expect to actually use them for guidance in funding decisions. No federal agency except HUD even required applicants to submit their CHAP when requesting funding, so these agencies never gave themselves the opportunity to see whether the funding requested really represented an overall state priority. Faced with several equally good proposals from one state and only able to fund half of them, a federal agency might have used the CHAPs to learn which localities needed the services most. However, federal agencies did not have this information. There was even some question on the part of respondents in this study as to whether HUD itself used the CHAPs when making decisions about its two non-formula programs, Transitional Housing and Permanent Housing for Handicapped Homeless Persons.

Other Barriers to Program Development. Barriers to program development range from basic perceptions about the nature and extent of the homeless problem to state constitutional restrictions, resistance of localities to housing development, and some very specific issues. Classic urban-rural conflicts and antagonisms come into play in some states when dealing with homelessness. From a rural perspective, homelessness is strictly an urban problem; from an urban perspective, rural areas do not provide any services, so rural homeless people may have to move to the cities. Rural areas may also "dump" homeless rural people on the big cities. Dumping can take the form of buying bus tickets for homeless people who cannot be accommodated in rural areas, or of escorting people in the local police car to just inside the city limits of cities with services for the homeless. Respondents in Georgia, New Mexico, and Wisconsin, among the states we visited, perceived that rural areas had a major influence in their state legislatures, and that traditional rural/urban political splits prevented a full commitment of state funds and energy to address homelessness. Program development, of course, suffers due to lack of resources.

Constitutional prohibitions on state funding of housing exist in both Ohio and Wisconsin, making it difficult to find an entity that can legally put together a housing development project and also has the technical skills and desire to do so. Proposition 13 constitutionally limits the State of California's taxing authority, with consequences for many government programs including those for the homeless. Constitutional requirements in Georgia bar giving state funds to religious entities; since most of the providers of homeless services in Georgia have a religious connection, this prohibition poses a substantial difficulty that requires a state constitutional amendment before certain programs can be activated. In Wisconsin, the governor constitutionally has a very powerful line item veto, which the incumbent has used to block a transitional housing program for the homeless, among many other items. This constitutional provision is also on the docket for amendment.

Perceptions from the Local Level

Although this review has chiefly focused on state activities as seen by state-level actors, we also sought from local government officials and service providers their perceptions of state and federal program support for homeless services and solutions to homelessness. Local officials and providers were contacted in one major city in each state (San Francisco, Hartford, Atlanta, Albuquerque, Cleveland, Milwaukee). This section describes local responses to questions about relations between local governments and providers and state agencies. These are often general, but sometimes pertain to specific laws, agency attitudes, or circumstances in the state in question.

General Perceptions of State-Local Relations. With the exception of Connecticut, local respondents indicated that their state governments did not provide overall state leadership on homeless issues, did not have an overview or comprehensive plan either for emergency services for all groups among the homeless or for serious prevention efforts, and were more responsive than proactive. In Connecticut local respondents *do* feel that the state government provides overall leadership on homeless issues. In Atlanta and Milwaukee, local coalitions of providers and activists supplied the leadership, often even after the McKinney Act. In Ohio, the statewide coalition did so. In four states, Georgia, New Mexico, Ohio, and Wisconsin, local respondents felt that the need to respond to the McKinney Act provisions has promoted more (or some) state government activity, including efforts at state-local communication and coordination.

Local respondents also mentioned specific widespread attitudes that made it difficult to find support for services for the homeless. Respondents in both Georgia and New Mexico mentioned statewide perceptions that the problem of homelessness was essentially concentrated in the state's largest city. Rural representatives to state legislatures were seen as using their influence to limit support for homeless programs. Local respondents in California, Ohio, and New Mexico mentioned that state agencies, legislators, and others in positions of power perceived the problem of homelessness largely in terms of the chronically mentally ill. Support for programs for other groups among the homeless (or even for chronically mentally ill homeless with other problems, such as substance abuse) was harder to obtain.

Specific Barriers Relating to Local-State Relations. Virtually all local (and some state) respondents mentioned that towns, municipalities, or neighborhoods often resisted the development of shelter or other emergency services on one hand, and transitional or permanent housing on the other. States, for their part, have mostly either not considered or have been unwilling to override local self-determination to require municipalities to shoulder their share of the burden. Cities with the largest homeless populations and the most services would prefer to see more services developed elsewhere around the state (to the point of offering technical assistance and even, in one instance, funding), to make it less necessary for homeless people to migrate from small towns to the major cities in search of services. Local respondents did not consider this likely to happen without strong state leadership, however.

In Ohio many providers support the Department of Mental Health's programmatic emphasis on permanent scattered site housing for the mentally ill, although the issue has sparked some controversy. *Scattered site* housing means a 10-unit housing project might own 10 apartments in 10 different buildings in 3 different neighborhoods, which housed 20 previously homeless individuals. However, because HUD favors the *group home concept* (that is, acquiring a single building and using it to house all 20 previously homeless individuals), local providers run into conflicts over this sharp philosophical difference when they try to design programs that would use both state and federal funds.

In New Mexico local providers report problems with the state's Mental Health Bureau, which is in the Department of Health and Environment. The Bureau sees the intent of the McKinney Act to provide service only to the chronically mentally ill--specifically schizophrenics who were deinstitutionalized in the last 20 years. However, if a service program limits itself to the chronically mentally ill, it places a severe limitation on services for people who may need mental health services to cope with the stresses and causes of homelessness, even though they do not have a severe mental illness. Currently, in Albuquerque, the public hospital has too few beds and only one transitional housing program exists for the mentally ill. The state wants Albuquerque providers to give services to the chronically mentally ill on an outpatient basis, although the providers perceive that their clients need more support than can be made available in this way. The state does not fund any mental health workers to go into shelters, and most shelter workers are ill equipped to deal with the mental health problems they encounter. Further, the state does not want the providers to use mental health funds to support any substance abuse counseling, even when a chronically mentally ill person may also be a substance abuser. The Mental Health Bureau has no responsibility for substance abuse, and the responsible department is not interested in funding services for the homeless.

Also in New Mexico, the Department of Health and Environment (HED) has traditionally not had much interaction with the city of Albuquerque. The city wants to gain more administrative say over state funds allocated to it, but HED is adamantly against relinquishing any control. The city of Albuquerque's relationship with the Department of Human Services is much better because that agency favors giving the local units more control.

In California, Proposition 13, the so-called "tax revolt" initiative of the early 1980s, continues to constrain state options. The June 1988 ballot contained an effort to change the spending limit (Proposition 71), but it was defeated. The spending limit puts a constraint on the legislative process, making it difficult to get new bills passed. According to one of the interviewees, the legislative process is so inadequate that advocates have resorted to ballot initiatives. Two such efforts, propositions 84 and 95, were described earlier.

Another California problem was posed by restrictions on building on flood plains. California law prohibits the placement of a shelter in a flood plain zone but, in some jurisdictions, large proportions of the land are in flood plain zones, severely restricting possibilities for emergency services. Providers feel that there are many ways to handle the flood danger, but remain stymied by this constraint. Also, slow growth policies in many California communities effectively prohibit low-income housing developments. California also requires that all workers be paid at least minimum wage. Thus persons cannot be hired in exchange for room and board and a small stipend if the stipend is less than what would be received if the minimum wage were paid.

In every state we learned of very state-specific and local-specific barriers to program development. We cite Georgia's list here to give the flavor of these sets of contraints, even though some specific items might change from state to state:

✦ In renovating city shelters using HUD funds, city contractors have to pay the Davis-Bacon wage rates. Atlanta is a non-unionized city, and to comply with the Davis-Bacon Act, contractors must pay a wage rate comparable to union wages for each industry involved. This has caused a problem for the city in using Community Development Block Grant funds.

✦ Fire codes, which are unevenly enforced, are unrealistic and costly for shelters. Fire codes and other standards seemed to be a statewide problem, especially with churches expanding into the shelter business after an initial intent to simply open a temporary shelter in the church's basement.

✦ In Atlanta, one provider mentioned the what he called "Inspector A and Inspector B" syndrome, where one inspector does a preliminary check and says everything is okay, and then another inspector comes in and cites numerous violations.

✦ Because HUD has categorized people with AIDS as diseased rather than handicapped, HUD money is not available for a shelter specifically for this population.

✦ There is little happening in the area of eviction protection and the law prohibits the Georgia Residential Finance Authority from using McKinney Act money for rehousing.

✦ It is difficult to leverage money from any source for the long-term issue of providing low cost housing. In part, this is seen as a perceptual problem in that the public thinks emergency shelters answer the need.

✦ Georgia has some particular problems in its service operation. For example, the average length of time to get food stamps through "expedited service" is 25 days, although legally it should be five days. There is no entity or procedure in place to handle complaints in this area.

✦ Within the city of Atlanta there are regulations regarding construction that make low-cost housing development extremely difficult. For instance, public utilities now require no-maintenance installations in new housing, which are quite expensive. Similarly the city requires high-cost, on-site piping installation and particular road specifications, which make the development of single family housing unprofitable. In the past year the city of Atlanta issued only 300 building permits compared with 5,000 apiece for each of the surrounding counties.

✦ The costs of risk and liability insurance and related complications are seen as preventing the service system from developing flexible non-traditional models.

✦ Reimbursement mechanisms, which require clear quantification of services, also impede creation of flexible systems.

✦ The prohibition of providing state funds to church-related organizations poses a problem in Georgia since the religious community leads in the response to homelessness.

✦ Catch-22's abound. For instance, although people are given Section 8 vouchers they may not be able to find affordable housing in Atlanta. The vouchers are valid for housing anywhere in the county, so people go outside the city for more reasonably priced housing and then find they have no transportation back to jobs, appointments, or services.

✦ Neighborhood coalitions resist the development of community residential facilities in their neighborhoods.

SUMMARY AND IMPLICATIONS

The six states visited in July 1988 display a wide variety of state-level programs and activities for the homeless, and very different levels of state commitment to address both emergency and preventive aspects of homelessness. Some states got organized around this issue relatively early in the decade; others still have no statewide organization or task force on the homeless. Some states spend considerable sums of their own money on programs for the homeless and take maximum advantage of available federal funds, while others spend practically no state funds and do not actively pursue federal dollars. Because our sample size is so limited, we cannot conduct statistical analyses of reasons for these differences--however, we did talk with at least 20 individuals in each of these states--from state agencies, local government, private agencies, and advocates. From these interviews we can summarize our impressions of some of the factors motivating state action or inhibiting involvement at the state level.

In general, government has been a latecomer in providing financial or programmatic support for homeless programs. Voluntary organizations--primarily missions, religious congregations, neighborhood coalitions, and charitable organizations--have led the way, developing both services and advocacy networks. The states in which government has done the most appear to be states with strong local voluntary services and statewide coalitions of service providers and advocates who have pressured government to act. These efforts have in turn developed as a response to the magnitude of the homeless problem in local communities. It appears that the more homeless there are in a community, and the more visible they are, the more services are developed, creating a stronger advocacy network.

The ability to mobilize strong statewide coalitions appears to depend on how widespread the problem is perceived to be throughout the state. The three states in our sample with one major population center in a largely rural/small-town state (Georgia, New Mexico, and Wisconsin) were also the states without a statewide coalition and with relatively little state involvement or commitment to address problems of homelessness. Conversely, the three states in our sample with numerous major population centers (California, Connecticut, and Ohio) had strong local networks, strong statewide coalitions, and major state involvement. This is not to say that the problem of homelessness is only an urban problem, but it does suggest that most people outside of urban areas perceive the problem that way. However, government and program officials in the cities, where most of the services are located, perceive that small towns and rural communities do not develop services for the homeless, who must then move to the cities. Rural communities may also occasionally "dump" their homeless people on the cities. These practices allow people outside of major population centers to ignore the problem of homelessness and to use their influence in state legislatures to deny state support for expanded services.

Another significant factor in Connecticut, and possibly also in California, is general inflation in the cost of housing at all levels. Connecticut officials candidly reported that the difficulty even middle- and upper-middle-income people in

Connecticut experienced in finding affordable housing had had two effects. First, legislators for many constituencies became aware of the affordable housing crunch and became willing to do something about it. Second, the Governor's Task Force recommendations (and consequently state policy) leaned heavily in the direction of longer-range planning for preventive actions. The task force directly addressed the issue of affordable housing through bond issues and various state programs for the development of low- and mixed-income housing throughout the state. In California inflation in the cost of housing and the consequent rise in property taxes (particularly in the Los Angeles and San Francisco areas, but elsewhere also) led the way to the state's well known taxpayers' revolt and Proposition 13 limiting tax increases. Politicians and advocates in California have recognized the need for serious efforts to provide affordable housing and voters have approved two large bond issues for that purpose (totalling $600 million) through the ballot initiative process.

Finally, the six states we visited differed in the level of sophistication of their state leadership. Connecticut has provided the strongest and most comprehensive leadership. The governor's commitment was clearly important here. He first created a statewide task force and charged it with considering long-range preventive needs as well as emergency needs. Next he followed up the task force recommendations by mandating coordination among state agencies and appointing a strong lead agency. He then assigned clear responsibilities for tasks and periodically evaluated progress on goals and objectives established by the state plan. In California and Ohio state leadership has not been as comprehensive. But in the area of assistance to the chronically mentally ill among the homeless, these two states have developed extensive and effective programs at multiple sites throughout the state. In the other three states visited, the relatively small and non-comprehensive level of program commitments clearly reflect the absence of real leadership with significant power at the state level.

Note, chapter 5

1. As the result of a law suit, the federal government had to compensate some states for excess energy expenses associated with oil from stripper wells.

Chapter Six

DIRECTIONS FOR FUTURE POLICY

From information gathered in the three research projects summarized in this report, one would have to conclude that the situation facing America's homeless is not good. Despite the efforts of providers to make the most of available resources, emergency food and shelter capacity meets only about half the need. Although some states are taking major initiatives around the problem of homelessness, great variation exists in approach, coordination, and levels of funding. How can we as a nation better address this situation?

A first step is to acknowledge the complexity of the causes of homelessness. Many factors have been cited as contributors to the growth of homelessness in the 1980s. The Committee on Intergovernmental Relations of the U.S. House of Representatives (1986) identified as causes of family homelessness the scarcity of low-income housing, inadequate income or public assistance benefits, increases in personal crises, and cuts in federal assistance programs. Several other factors mentioned by the media as probably related to increased homelessness are increases in the numbers of people in poverty, deinstitutionalization and other mental health policies, changes in the labor market (away from manufacturing and toward service industries), the low level of the minimum wage, and, an increase in single-parent families. Housing factors cited include the destruction or conversion of single room occupancy and other very inexpensive housing, housing inflation outpacing wage increases in certain major U.S. housing markets, and shifts in government policy regarding the financing of low-income housing development.

The variety of these factors implies that the causes of homelessness cannot simply be attributed to the actions or inactions of one sector of society--neither the federal government, other governments, or the private sector. Similarly, the solutions to homelessness will not emerge from only one sector.

The experience of the states and local governments most involved in developing solutions to homelessness suggests that a multiplicity of approaches is needed. Solutions must be sought at three levels: the emergency response, transitional programs, and prevention. Emergency services provide food, shelter, and health care to people already homeless. These are the best developed services to date; they have largely been supported, on a shoestring, by the nonprofit sector and by religious organizations and congregations. Only in the last two to three years has government provided significant support for most of these programs.

(Transitional programs help people already homeless to get back into permanent housing, and most important, to develop a greater capacity for self-sufficiency. Most of these programs are still in their infancy, and serve only a fraction of homeless individuals and families.) The structures and activities of transitional programs are limited only by the ingenuity of the service providers who directly observe the needs of their clients and work to create supportive programs and services tailored to those needs. However, transitional programs frequently involve literacy training, job training, chemical dependency treatment, mental health treatment, money management assistance, child care, transportation, and other specialized services. Such services require substantially higher cash investments than do emergency services, which frequently rely heavily on volunteers. The lack of these services, despite clear need, is testimony to the limits of the voluntary sector in meeting the entire scope of the needs of the homeless.

Prevention approaches are even less developed than transitional programs. Ideally, public policy should strive to keep people from becoming homeless in the first place, either by bringing down the cost of housing, by increasing the personal resources of poor people, or both. To a much greater degree than for emergency services, creating enough affordable housing is a challenge for the whole society, requiring the combined ingenuity of government, nonprofit agencies, and the housing industry. The federal government will probably be called upon to act primarily as a source of funds--either through direct grants or through tax incentives. The major current federal mechanism for supporting homeless programs, the McKinney Act, clearly needs to smooth out some conceptual and administrative difficulties in order to fulfill its promise in areas other than support for building or renovating emergency shelters. State and local governments will also be expected to provide funding for services. These governments should also play a major role in planning and coordinating services. The housing industry will have to be involved in actually building or renovating housing.

Examples of sophisticated and innovative low-income housing developments already exist. In Pittsburgh a for-profit developer renovated an old downtown YMCA. The developer preserved and upgraded the Y's SRO housing, rented two floors to county social services and mental health agencies (for income and to bring services close to building residents), and used historical preservation tax credits as part of the financing package (Mistik 1988). In Boston another for-profit developer renovates old boarding houses to create group housing that single individuals working in minimum wage jobs can afford (O'Malley 1988). In Los Angeles the Single Room Occupancy Housing Corporation, a nonprofit developer, has renovated 11 old downtown hotels to provide permanent housing for previously homeless individuals. In these hotels, floors are set aside to provide specialized services for people with particular needs, such as the elderly and the chronically mentally ill. The corporation also helped develop a local park, participated in a voter registration drive, sponsored a job fair, and serves as a food bank distribution site, to build a sense of community in the downtown neighborhood (Raubeson 1988). And in San Francisco the nonprofit Bridge Housing Corporation is building housing units renting at under $400 a month for low-income families, using a combination of land purchased from, and then leased back, to the city. The building is financed with tax-increment bonds, negotiated reduced interest rates on commercial loans, and corporate financing, in exchange for tax credits for investment in very low-income housing (Terner 1988). Under present financing options, including those available through federal legislation, creating the financing package for such projects requires incredible perseverance and sophistication, but it can be done. More and more organizations, both for-profit and not-for-profit, are recognizing the need and responding.

Finally, it will be essential for the voluntary sector to continue its commitment, innovativeness, and advocacy. As in the past, the voluntary sector will supply the largest proportion of day-to-day work addressing the needs of the homeless. The voluntary sector will have to continue its key advocacy role--keeping the heat on government and voters to develop the policies and resources necessary to find solutions to the plight of America's homeless.

The data in the report show that--despite great growth of services in the 1980s and the efforts of providers--today's levels of resources are not meeting the need. It suggests that public policy concerning homelessness is far from strong at the federal level and unevenly developed among the states.

There is evidence that a breakdown has occurred in this country in the basic systems that are supposed to keep the populace from complete impoverishment. The national estimates of the number of homeless people in this report make it difficult to maintain that homelessness is a local problem, to be addressed by affected cities with little help from federal or state governments. With an estimated 500,000 to 600,000 homeless Americans at any given time, homelessness has emerged as a national problem of serious proportions.

REFERENCES

Appelbaum, Richard. 1985a. Testimony and Prepared Statement, Hearing Before the Subcommittee on Housing and Community Development of the Committee on Banking, Finance and Urban Affairs, House of Representatives, 98th Congress, 2nd session, May 24, 1984, Serial No. 99-56: *HUD Report on Homelessness - I.*

Appelbaum, Richard. 1985b. Testimony and Prepared Statement, Hearing Before the Subcommittee on Housing and Community Development of the Committee on Banking, Finance and Urban Affairs, House of Representatives, 99th Congress, 1st session, December 4, 1985, Serial No. 99-56: *HUD Report on Homelessness - II, pp. 7-41.*

Brown, Carl, Steve MacFarlane, Ron Paredes, and Louisa Stark. 1983. *The Homeless of Phoenix: Who are They and What should be Done?* Phoenix, Ariz.: Phoenix South Community Mental Health Center.

Burt, Martha R. 1988. Projections of Our Estimate of Service-using Homeless People in U.S. Cities of 100,000 or More to All Homeless People in the United States. Urban Institute Memorandum submitted to Food and Nutrition Service, U.S. Department of Agriculture, September 11, 1988.

Burt, Martha R. and Barbara E. Cohen. 1988a. *Review of Research on Homeless Persons.* Washington, D.C.: The Urban Institute. Report submitted to the Food and Nutrition Service, U.S. Department of Agriculture, and the Interagency Council on the Homeless.

Burt, Martha R. and Barbara E. Cohen. 1988b. *Feeding the Homeless: Does the Prepared Meals Provision Help?* Washington, D.C.: The Urban Institute. Report prepared for the Food and Nutrition Service, U.S. Department of Agriculture and submitted to Congress October 31, 1988.

Burt, Martha R. and Barbara E. Cohen. 1988c. *State Programs and Activities for the Homeless: A Review of Six States.* Washington, D.C.: The Urban Institute.

Burt, Martha R. and Lynn C. Burbridge. 1985. *Summary, Conclusions and Recommendations: Evaluation of the Emergency Food and Shelter Program.* Washington, D.C.: The Urban Institute.

City of Boston Emergency Shelter Commission. 1983. "The October Project: Seeing the Obvious Problem." Boston, Mass.

City of Boston. 1986. "Making Room: Comprehensive Policy for the Homeless." Boston, Mass.

Committee for Food and Shelter, Inc. 1987. "Characteristics and Housing Needs of the Homeless." Washington, D.C.

Committee on Intergovernmental Relations, U.S. House of Representatives. 1986. "Homeless Families: A Neglected Crisis." Washington, D.C.: USGPO, House Report 99-982.

Department of Housing and Urban Development. 1984. *A Report to the Secretary on the Homeless and Emergency Shelters.* Washington, D.C.: Department of Housing and Urban Development, Office of Policy Development and Research.

Department of Housing and Urban Development. 1989. *A Report on the 1988 National Survey of Shelters for the Homeless.* Washington, D.C.: Department of Housing and Urban Development, Office of Policy Development and Research.

Dietz, Stephen. 1985. Letter dated July 23, 1985, from Stephen Dietz to Jack Anderson with attachments. Hearing Before the Subcommittee on Housing and Community Development of the Committee on Banking, Finance and Urban Affairs, House of Representatives, 99th Congress, 1st session, December 4, 1985, Serial No. 99-56: *HUD Report on Homelessness - II,* pp. 92-99.

Farr, Rodger K., Paul Koegel, and Audrey Burnam. 1986. *A Study of Homelessness and Mental Illness in the Skid Row Area of Los Angeles.* Los Angeles, Calif.: Los Angeles County Department of Mental Health.

Food and Nutrition Service, USDA. 1987. *A Study of the Temporary Emergency Food Assistance Program: Report to Congress.* Washington, D.C.: USDA.

Freeman, Richard B. and Brian Hall. 1987. "Permanent Homelessness in America?" *Population Research and Policy Review,* vol. 6, pp. 3-27.

General Accounting Office. 1988. *Homeless Mentally Ill: Problems and Options in Estimating Numbers and Trends.* Washington, D.C.: GAO/RCED-88-63.

General Accounting Office. 1987. *Homelessness: Implementation of Food and Shelter Programs Under the McKinney Act.* Washington, D.C.: U.S. General Accounting Office, GAO/RCED-88-63.

Goplerud, Eric. 1987. "Homelessness in Fairfax County: Needs Assessment of Homeless Persons and Implications for Programs and Policies." Fairfax, Va.: George Mason University.

Hirschl, Thomas and Jamshid A. Momeni. 1988. "Homelessness in New York: A Demographic and Socioeconomic Analysis." Paper presented at the Population Association of America Annual Meeting, New Orleans, April 1988.

Human Nutrition Information Service, USDA. 1986. "Nutrition and Your Health, Dietary Guidelines for Americans: Eat a Variety of Foods." Home and Garden Bulletin #232-1. Hyattsville, MD: HNIS-USDA, April 1986, p. 3.

Human Nutrition Information Service, USDA. 1980. *Food Intakes and Nutrients, Individuals in One Day in the U.S., Spring 1977.* Preliminary Report #2. Hyattsville, MD: HNIS-USDA, September 1980.

King County Department of Planning and Community Development. 1986. *Homelessness Revisited: 1986 Seattle-King County Emergency Shelter Study Update.* Seattle, Wash.: King County Department of Planning and Community Development, Housing and Community Development Division.

Lee, Barrett A. 1988. "Stability and Change in an Urban Homeless Population." Nashville, Tenn.: Vanderbilt University. Paper presented at Population Association of America Annual Meeting, 1988.

Mathematica Policy Research. 1987. *Final Report for the Food and Nutrition Service, USDA: Descriptive Tables Based Upon Merged Wave 1 Data for the Essential and Low-Income Samples of the 1985 CSFII*. Washington, D.C.

Mistik, D. Thomas. 1988. Presentation at National Association of Home Builders conference, Builders Examine the Many Faces of Homelessness, session on "Single Room Occupancy Housing: A Revitalization Underway."

Mowbray, Carol T., V. Sue Johnson, Andrea Solarz and Claudia J. Combs. 1985. "Mental Health and Homelessness in Detroit: A Research Study." East Lansing, Mich.: Michigan Department of Mental Health.

Mulkern, Virginia, Valerie J. Bradley, Rebecca Spence, Susan Allein, and John E. Oldham. 1985. *Homelessness Needs Assessment Study: Findings and Recommendations for the Massachusetts Department of Mental Health*. Boston, Mass.: Human Services Research Institute.

Multnomah County Social Service Division. 1984. "The Homeless Poor." Multnomah County (Portland), Oreg.

Multnomah County Social Services Division. 1985. "Homeless Women." Multnomah County (Portland), Oreg.

National Research Council. 1980. *Recommended Dietary Allowances*, 9th ed., rev. Washington, D.C.: National Academy Press.

O'Malley, Marjorie. 1988. Presentation at National Association of Home Builders conference, Builders Examine the Many Faces of Homelessness, session on "Single Room Occupancy Housing: A Revitalization Underway."

Piliavin, Irving, Michael Sosin, and Herb Westerfelt. 1987. "Tracking the Homeless." *Focus,* vol. 10, no. 4, Winter 1987-1988, pp. 20-5. Madison, Wis.: University of Wisconsin-Madison Institute for Research on Poverty.

Raubeson, Andy. 1988. Presentation at National Association of Home Builders conference, Builders Examine the Many Faces of Homelessness, session on "Single Room Occupancy Housing: A Revitalization Underway."

Robinson, Frederic. 1985. "Homeless People in The Nation's Capital." Washington, D.C.: University of the District of Columbia.

Ropers, Richard and Marjorie Robertson. 1985. "Basic Shelter Research Project. Report #4." Los Angeles, Calif.: UCLA School of Public Health.

Rosnow, Mark J., Toni Shaw, and Clare Stapleton Concord. 1985. "A Study of Homeless Mentally Ill Persons in Milwaukee." Milwaukee, Wis.: Human Services Triangle, Inc.

Rossi, Peter H., Gene A. Fisher, and Georgianna Willis. 1986. *The Condition of the Homeless in Chicago.* Amherst, Mass.: Social and Demographic Research Institute, University of Massachusetts; Chicago, Ill.: National Opinion Research Center (NORC).

Roth, Dee, Jerry Bean, Nancy Just, and Traian Saveanu. 1985. *Homelessness in Ohio: A Study of People in Need.* Columbus, Ohio: Ohio Department of Mental Health, Office of Program Evaluation and Research.

Task Force on Emergency Shelter. 1983. "Homelessness in Chicago." Chicago, Ill: Task Force on Emergency Shelter, Social Services Task Force, Department of Human Services, City of Chicago.

Terner, Don. 1988. Presentation at National Association of Home Builders conference, Builders Examine the Many Faces of Homelessness, session on "Creative Financing: A Key to Housing the Homeless."

United States Conference of Mayors. 1987. "A Status Report on Homeless Families in America's Cities." Washington, D.C.

United States Conference of Mayors. 1986a. "The Continued Growth of Hunger, Homelessness and Poverty in America's Cities: 1986." Washington, D.C., December.

United States Conference of Mayors. 1986b. "The Growth of Hunger, Homelessness and Poverty in America's Cities." Washington, D.C., January.

United States Conference of Mayors. 1984. "Homelessness in America's Cities." Washington, D.C.

U.S. Department of Health and Human Services and U.S. Department of Agriculture. 1986. *Nutrition Monitoring in the United States -- A Report from the Joint Nutrition Monitoring Evaluation Committee.* DHHS Publication No. (PHS) 86-1255. Washington, D.C.: US Government Printing Office.

Vernez, Georges, M. Audrey Burnam, Elizabeth A. McGlynn, Sally Trude, and Brian Mittman. 1988. *Review of California's Program for the Homeless Mentally Disabled.* Santa Monica, Calif.: The Rand Corporation.

Weigand, Bruce. 1985. "Counting the Homeless: Nashville, Tennessee." *American Demographics,* December.

Winograd, Kenneth. 1983. "Street People and Other Homeless: Pittsburgh Study." Pittsburgh, Pa.: Emergency Shelter Task Force, Allegheny County MH/MR/DA Program.

Woods, William K. and Edward L. Burdell. 1987. "Homelessness in Cincinnati." Cincinnati, Ohio: Applied Information Resources.

Wright, James and Eleanor Weber. 1987. *Homelessness and Health*. Washington, D.C.: McGraw-Hill's Healthcare Information Center.